The Ladykillers

by Graham Linehan

From the Motion Picture Screenplay
by William Rose

By Special Arrangement with Studio Canal

& By Special Arrangement with
Fiery Angel Ltd, London

A SAMUEL FRENCH ACTING EDITION

FOUNDED 1830

SAMUELFRENCH.COM
SAMUELFRENCH-LONDON.CO.UK

FOR PRODUCTION ENQUIRIES

UNITED STATES AND CANADA

Info@SamuelFrench.com

1-866-598-8449

UNITED KINGDOM AND EUROPE

Plays@SamuelFrench-London.co.uk

020-7255-4302

Each title is subject to availability from Samuel French, depending upon country of performance. Please be aware that *THE LADYKILLERS* may not be licensed by Samuel French in your territory. Professional and amateur producers should contact the nearest Samuel French office or licensing partner to verify availability.

THE LADYKILLERS
By Graham Linehan
From the motion picture screenplay by William Rose
By special arrangement with StudioCanal
& by special arrangement with Fiery Angel Ltd, London

Original West End Production
Gielgud Theatre, London
Official Opening Night 7 December 2011

Presented by Edward Snape for Fiery Angel
in association with Stage Entertainment UK, Fiery Dragons, Olympus Theatricals,
StudioCanal, Jason Haigh-Ellery & Liverpool Everyman & Playhouse

Direction — Sean Foley
Set and Costume Design — Michael Taylor
Lighting Design — James Farncombe Composition & Sound Design — Ben & Max Ringham
Special Effects Design — Scott Penrose Casting — Sarah Bird CDG
Script Associate — Sean Foley Associate Director — Nicola Samer
Associate Sound Designer — Simon Moloney Fight Direction — Alison De Burgh

Cast (in order of appearance)

Constable Macdonald	Harry Peacock
Mrs Louisa Wilberforce	Marcia Warren
Professor Marcus	Peter Capaldi
Major Courtney	James Fleet
Harry Robinson	Stephen Wight
One-Round	Clive Rowe
Louis Harvey	Ben Miller
Mrs Jane Tromleyton	Beverley Walding
Company/understudies	Marcus Taylor, William Troughton and Lace Akpojaro

General Management — Jon Bath and Sarah Davies for Fiery Angel Ltd
Production Management — Crosbie Marlow Associates
Company Stage Manager — Marcus Watson
Deputy Stage Manager — Briony Allen
Assistant Stage Managers — Jason Mills, Elizabeth Webster and Nadia Luijten
Costume Supervisor — Sue Coates
Props Supervisor — Robin Morgan
Make Up and Hair Supervisor — Jenny Glynn
Wardrobe Mistress — Caroline Bromley
Wardrobe Assistant — Kieron Stone

MUSIC USE NOTE

Licensees are solely responsible for obtaining formal written permission from copyright owners to use copyrighted music in the performance of this play and are strongly cautioned to do so. If no such permission is obtained by the licensee, then the licensee must use only original music that the licensee owns and controls. Licensees are solely responsible and liable for all music clearances and shall indemnify the copyright owners of the play(s) and their licensing agent, Samuel French, against any costs, expenses, losses and liabilities arising from the use of music by licensees. Please contact the appropriate music licensing authority in your territory for the rights to any incidental music.

IMPORTANT BILLING AND CREDIT REQUIREMENTS

If you have obtained performance rights to this title, please refer to your licensing agreement for important billing and credit requirements.

VIDEO-RECORDING

Please note that the copyright laws governing video-recording are extremely complex and that it should not be assumed that any play may be video-recorded for whatever purpose without first obtaining the permission of the appropriate agents. The fact that a play is published by Samuel French Ltd does not indicate that video rights are available or that Samuel French Ltd controls such rights.

CHARACTERS

Constable Macdonald
Mrs Louisa Wilberforce
Professor Marcus
Major Courtney
Harry Robinson
One-Round
Louis Harvey
Mrs Jane Tromleyton
Mrs Wilberforce's Guests

The action takes place in King's Cross, London, from 5th to 9th November 1956

ACT I
ACT II

GRAHAM LINEHAN

Graham Linehan is an Irish comedy writer and director, as well as an actor and comedian, and creator of highly popular series *Father Ted*, *The IT Crowd* and *Black Books*.

After an early career as a journalist for the Irish music magazine *Hot Press*, Graham began collaborating with writer Arthur Mathews on many high profile comedy sketch shows including *Alas Smith and Jones*, *Harry Enfield and Chums*, and the Ted and Ralph characters in *The Fast Show*.

It was Linehan and Matthews' creation of *Father Ted* in 1995 that brought their greatest success of their early years. The programme won countless awards, including two BAFTAs for best comedy, and is today regarded as one of the greatest British sitcoms ever produced.

Linehan and Matthews then wrote the first series of the sketch show *Big Train*, which Graham also directed.

Linehan has since written for other shows, including *Brass Eye*. 2000 saw his next success with his co-creation of *Black Books* with Dylan Moran. Graham also co-directed many episodes with Nick Wood.

In 2003 Graham directed the pilot episode of *Little Britain*.

Linehan went on to create, write and direct the 2006 Channel 4 sitcom *The IT Crowd*, starring Chris O'Dowd and Richard Ayoade, which went on to win multiple awards including the BAFTA TV Award for 'Best Situation Comedy' in 2009, 'Best TV Sitcom' at the British Comedy Awards in 2009, and 'Best Script for Television' at the Irish Film and Television Awards.

Over the last ten years Graham has also directed numerous ad campaigns with Sneezing Tree Films, including campaigns for ITV Sports Channel, which were awarded the Silver Arrow at the 2003 BTAA Awards, and four commercials from the award winning QTV series starring Martin Freeman. He directed the IKEA 'Van de Poop' campaign and in 2011 he did the Direct Line campaign starring Chris Addison, Alexander Armstrong and Amelia Bulmore.

Most recently, in November 2011, Graham's stage adaptation of the Ealing Studio classic *The Ladykillers* debuted at The Liverpool Playhouse before moving to The Gielgud Theatre, London starring Peter Capaldi and Ben Miller, where it broke box-office records and received rave reviews.

WILLIAM ROSE

Born in Missouri in 1918, Bill Rose escaped to New York, where he did a series of very odd jobs, and from there joined the Canadian Black Watch (RHR) as a volunteer in 1940. While stationed in England during the war he met and married an English wife and at the end of the war decided to settle there. His first opportunity to write for the screen came in 1949 as a Trainee Screenwriter at Pinewood Studios. His first original story and screenplay was *Genevieve* (1953). Altogether he wrote seventeen films, of which the best remembered, apart from *Genevieve*, are probably *The Ladykillers* (1954) and *Guess Who's Coming to Dinner* (1967) for which he won an Oscar.

Although often associated with Ealing Studios he only wrote four films for them, three of which were not comedies. He later wrote five films for American producers of which the best remembered, apart from *Guess* are probably *It's a Mad, Mad, Mad, Mad World* (1962) and *The Russians are Coming, the Russians are Coming* (1966). He died in 1987.

ACT I

The exterior of a house

We hear snatches of street sounds, birdsong, and regular steam trains going past, with their whistles and screeching

As the HOUSE LIGHTS GO DOWN...

A portly bobby, CONSTABLE MACDONALD, wanders up along the street to the house, whistling

He pauses outside the house to pick up a bottle of milk on the doorstep

He knocks at the door, it is opened by an sweet little old woman, MRS. WILBERFORCE. He goes inside, and on the same beat as she closes the door shut...

MUSIC FILLS THE AIR, AS...

THE SET SLOWLY REVOLVES...

To reveal...

A QUINTESSENTIAL ENGLISH DRAWING ROOM

Florid wallpaper, chintzy furnishing. But everything slightly wonky. This is a house with extreme subsidence of many and various kinds

AS THE MUSIC STILL PLAYS...

We see CONSTABLE MACDONALD is now sitting opposite MRS. WILBERFORCE

They are drinking tea

THE MUSIC IS COMING TO AN END, AS...

THE SET COMPLETES ITS REVOLVE, AS...

On the last beat of the music, MRS. WILBERFORCE puts her teacup on her saucer with a... 'TING!'

****

CONSTABLE MACDONALD Mister Evans?
MRS. WILBERFORCE Yes.
CONSTABLE MACDONALD Mister Evans from...from down the... Mister Evans the newsagent?
MRS. WILBERFORCE Yes.
CONSTABLE MACDONALD Moustache. The Mister Evans with the moustache?
MRS. WILBERFORCE Yes. Goodness, Constable!
CONSTABLE MACDONALD I do apologise, M'm. It's just... It's quite an accusation.
MRS. WILBERFORCE Nevertheless. There it is.
CONSTABLE MACDONALD Crikey.

He takes up his notebook

CONSTABLE MACDONALD (CONT'D) All right, Mrs. Wilberforce... let's begin at the beginning. What exactly was it that first led you to believe that Mister Evans was a high-ranking Nazi?
MRS. WILBERFORCE Well...
CONSTABLE MACDONALD I mean, if I may... it could be argued that someone from Hitler's cabinet would be... so well known in England... that it would be a bit of an unusual move to open a newsagents in King's Cross.
MRS. WILBERFORCE Yes, you see? It's the last thing we would expect!
CONSTABLE MACDONALD Right... So, what was it about him that first aroused your suspicions? Was it some sort of gesture? Was he perhaps reaching for something?

He demonstrates by doing a 'reaching-for-something'/Nazi salute gesture

MRS. WILBERFORCE No, but you must admit his accent is very unusual. Like someone trying to strangle or suppress his own, natural German accent.
CONSTABLE MACDONALD He's from Burnley.
MRS. WILBERFORCE Also, the other day, I was performing an errand, and he seemed very interested in gaining directions to my home.

CONSTABLE MACDONALD Yes, but... again, forgive me, but... why would a former Nazi be after that information?

MRS. WILBERFORCE Ah, you see, just before the war, I wrote several letters to The Times criticizing the German leaders for their terrible aggression. They really were quite unpleasant.

CONSTABLE MACDONALD The letters?

MRS. WILBERFORCE The Nazis. I thought perhaps a spirit of revenge might motivate Mister Evans in wishing me ill. This urgent need to find the exact position of my house ... This is the crux of the matter, Constable... he was quite insistent...

CONSTABLE MACDONALD Yes ...

MRS. WILBERFORCE .. and created what I felt was an unnecessary scene. I had to subdue him with my umbrella.

CONSTABLE MACDONALD Yes, he sounded subdued on the phone. But, Mrs. Wilberforce, weren't you... with the greatest respect... hadn't you asked him to put up a notification that you were letting out a room? Perhaps that was why he wanted the directions? So that he could put it on the card?

She stares at him

Mrs. Wilberforce seems, all of a sudden, lost

MRS. WILBERFORCE Oh, Constable... You must think me a terrible fool.

CONSTABLE MACDONALD Nooooo!

MRS. WILBERFORCE I really must go and apologise...

CONSTABLE MACDONALD I shall do so on your behalf.

He gets up to leave

There is a sudden SQUAWK. It seems to be coming from underneath a COVERED BIRD CAGE

GENERAL GORDON *Stay for tea!!*

MRS. WILBERFORCE General Gordon, shush!

GENERAL GORDON *Please stay for tea!!*

MRS. WILBERFORCE General! You naughty boy!

GENERAL GORDON *You naughty boy!! Braaak!!*

CONSTABLE MACDONALD Now, I don't want you to feel embarrassed, Mrs. Wilberforce. We're grateful for your vigilance, we really are. If you'd just try to ... eliminate the likely before you arrive at things like Hitler and space aliens.

MRS.WILBERFORCE That was not my fault! How was I supposed to
  know that Mrs.Tromleyton was describing a... a radio play?
CONSTABLE MACDONALD It's just we had a quite a few officers
  out on that one. And it was FA Cup night.
MRS.WILBERFORCE Oh, Constable.
CONSTABLE MACDONALD Now, now, Mrs. Wilberforce, it's not a
  problem in the least. Just bear in mind what I said.
MRS. WILBERFORCE Thank you, Constable. I do wonder if your
  colleagues would be nearly so patient with me.
CONSTABLE MACDONALD Well... you're not on their beat.

They go to the door

CONSTABLE MACDONALD (CONT'D) Goodbye, Mrs. Wilberforce!
MRS. WILBERFORCE Goodbye, Constable! Thank you again!

He leaves

There is a sudden SQUAWK from under the cover of the birdcage

GENERAL GORDON Squawk! Please stay for tea! Please stay for tea!
MRS. WILBERFORCE Oh, shush, General Gordon. No-one wants to
  listen to a silly old bird going on...

She stops short

MRS. WILBERFORCE (CONT'D) Well!

*She gets up and picks up the tea tray. She walks to the kitchen, and over
to the sink which has a mysterious cluster of pipes above it. She picks
up a hammer, turns on the tap and then BANGS THE HELL OUT OF
THE PIPES*

SFX Pipes

*Suddenly, a black SHADOW looms at the back of the house. Someone
is watching her. The SHADOW creeps up the wall, getting larger and
larger until...*

DING DONG — the silliest, least threatening doorbell sound rings out

SFX Ding Dong

MRS. WILBERFORCE (CONT'D) Oh!

She crosses to the door and opens it...

... revealing a SINISTER figure. He takes off his hat with utmost respect and exaggeratedly SMILES.

MARCUS Mrs. Wilberforce?
MRS. WILBERFORCE Yes?...
MARCUS My name is Marcus. I believe you have rooms to let.
MRS. WILBERFORCE What...but...who told you?
MARCUS A very shaken newsagent.
    (*hands her a card*)
    May I come in?
MRS. WILBERFORCE Oh... Yes! Do! Come in! Oh, my goodness!

He slinks in and takes his first look at the house, sizing it up in a suddenly serious way

Mrs. Wilberforce is in a complete tizzy

MARCUS How marvellous to have such a splendid house all to yourself!
MRS. WILBERFORCE Oh, I'm not quite alone!
MARCUS Really?
MRS. WILBERFORCE Would you like some tea, Mister Marcus?
MARCUS Professor.
MRS. WILBERFORCE Oh! I do apologise, I should have known! Professor Marcus!
MARCUS I wouldn't want to put you to any trouble, Mrs. Wilberforce.
MRS. WILBERFORCE It's certainly no trouble! Do you take sugar?
MARCUS Just a suspicion, thank you. When you say, not quite alone...

She leads him into the living room. She disappears into the kitchen

MRS. WILBERFORCE Oh, I suppose I'm being silly. I only meant General Gordon.
MARCUS General Gordon?

Marcus looks around for this 'General Gordon'

MRS. WILBERFORCE Yes. But please, do ignore him.
MARCUS I will if I can find him...

Marcus looks at the URN underneath a portrait of a HANDSOME SEA CAPTAIN

MARCUS (CONT'D) Oh, I see! Is this him in here?

MRS. WILBERFORCE Yes, I have to keep him in there. He has a terribly rare condition that means he cannot be exposed to direct sunlight. And he's not very good with company.

Marcus stares at the urn, totally confused. He backs away, not noticing the parrot's cage he's backing into

MARCUS What's he likely to do? If he's uncovered?

MRS. WILBERFORCE Well, you know. Jump out at you and shriek.

Marcus nervously walks backwards from the urn and bumps into GENERAL GORDON'S CAGE

SQUAWK!

Marcus gets a terrible shock

MARCUS Ahhhhhh!

MRS. WILBERFORCE (*from the kitchen*) You see? Shush, General Gordon!

GENERAL GORDON Squawk! Please stay for tea!

MRS. WILBERFORCE Pay no attention to him, Professor. He's a dreadful old moaning minnie. General Gordon, do be quiet!

Marcus calms down in a furious way

GENERAL GORDON Squawk! Please stay for tea! Squawwwwwwk! SQUAWWWWWK!

Marcus, composed now, walks slowly over to the cage as the parrot continues and draws the cover up. We don't see the parrot, but Marcus does and the sight shocks him.

MARCUS Good God.

MRS. WILBERFORCE I do apologise for his behaviour. In the future, I will ensure that you are not disturbed by him.

MARCUS Well, he is disturbing. That's certainly some condition! He looks like a diseased washing up glove.

MRS. WILBERFORCE Would that it were only his appearance affected, Professor. The condition is... that is to say... he has only a short time left on this realm.

MARCUS Ah.
MRS. WILBERFORCE Yes. There is a veterinarian in America working
on an experimental treatment...
MARCUS So there is some hope?
MRS. WILBERFORCE ...but such an expedition would be far beyond
my means.
MARCUS Oh. So, "no".
MRS. WILBERFORCE I'm afraid there's nothing that can be done.

Pause

MARCUS Any chance we could have a look at the room?
MRS. WILBERFORCE Of course! Oh, forgive me.
MARCUS Nothing to forgive, Mrs. Wilberforce. You were miles away
with your diseased cockatoo.

*She starts up the stairs and turns on a light, revealing the FIRST FLOOR
LANDING*

UPSTAIRS...

MRS. WILBERFORCE I feel I should say, I can't provide breakfast or
early morning tea.
MARCUS I don't care.

She swings open the door to the rooms

MARCUS (CONT'D) (*immediately*) I'll take it!

*He starts down the stairs, almost dancing down them. Mrs. Wilberforce
trails behind*

MRS. WILBERFORCE Oh, ah, don't you want to see the rest of the
house?

DOWNSTAIRS...

MARCUS No need, Mrs. Wilberforce! The room is perfect! Quite
perfect!
MRS. WILBERFORCE (*still coming down*) Really? I was concerned
with the train tracks being so...
MARCUS Convenient? No, no, I enjoy trains. I'm often at the station
with my little notebook.

MRS. WILBERFORCE I should tell you that the house does have its
idiosyncrasies — if you turn the light off in the bathroom, for example,
all the other lights go out.
MARCUS Charming! Character!

*He corrects a skew-whiff picture on the wall. It immediately swings back
into its original position*

MARCUS (CONT'D) Ha, ha! That's slightly annoying, though, isn't
it?
MRS. WILBERFORCE I have subsidence.
MARCUS Do you? Oh, the house, I see. Bomb damage?
MRS. WILBERFORCE Yes, I believe my house was targeted
deliberately. Before the war, you see, I wrote a series of strong letters
to the —
MARCUS Plenty of time to catch up later, Mrs. Wilberforce! We are to
be housemates, after all!
MRS. WILBERFORCE Oh, yes!

Marcus continues to try and right the painting as he speaks...

MARCUS Now, one thing. I am part of a small musical group...
MRS. WILBERFORCE Oh, you're a Professor of Music!

The picture slips... he puts it back

MARCUS No, no, no, no. Merely a keen amateur!

The picture again...

MARCUS (CONT'D) But we were hoping for somewhere to practise.
MRS. WILBERFORCE Practise? Here? Oh, but... but that would be
simply wonderful, Professor!

The picture again — it stays...

MARCUS Marvellous! So unusual to find a person of discernment in
North London.
MRS. WILBERFORCE I should be happy, should you require one, to
act as... as an ear, as it were.
MARCUS As an ear? Ah, no, thank you, no need. We're fine for ears.
In fact, privacy is our main requirement, Mrs. Wilberforce! We could
never be disturbed while in rehearsal "mode".

MRS. WILBERFORCE Of course! It was quite inappropriate for me to suggest being an ear.

MARCUS (*he moves away*) You see, Mrs. Wilberforce, while I hesitate to —

Marcus jerks back slightly. Mrs. Wilberforce is standing on his scarf. Marcus gently attempts to pluck it from under her feet

MARCUS (CONT'D) Sorry, if I may... ah...

MRS. WILBERFORCE Yes?

She doesn't notice his difficulty. After a moment, he manages to jerk it away, and he staggers back slightly

MARCUS Ha. While I hesitate to describe ourselves as artists — artists such as my companions and I — need absolute serenity in order to work effectively... peace and quiet is what I crave... can you provide it?

MRS. WILBERFORCE Oh, absolutely, Professor!

There is a rumbling sound....

SFX Train

...as a TRAIN passes close to the house. It shakes the entire building... crockery rattles, the tassles on the lamps jitter and dance, the LIGHTS FLICKER ON AND OFF, PLUNGING THE STAGE INTO COMPLETE DARKNESS

For the length of time it takes to pass, it is BEDLAM

Beneath all this, Marcus continues to talk to Mrs. Wilberforce

The train rumbles off into the distance and the lights flicker back on

MARCUS You've convinced me!

SFX Whistle

Mrs. Wilberforce takes his hand, just as the painting slips and swings back to its cockeyed position

****

MUSIC... LIGHT CHANGE... A NEW DAY...

Darkness

In amongst the sounds of the creaking house and distant trains, we hear the crackle of the radio, and the measured voice of a BBC news announcer...

NEWSREADER   The Prime Minister has today announced that British Forces will be deployed alongside their French counterparts in an International police action to secure the Suez Canal. Operation Musketeer is in response to the Egyptian nationalisation of the Canal, announced in July by President Nasser. The Prime Minister...

Light slowly spills into the house. The spare room has a lived-in look. Bed unmade, coat thrown over a chair etc. There is also a small radio on the floor

The sound of the W.C. flushing. From inside it, we hear Marcus singing the tune of Boccherini's Minuet. He swings the door of the lavvy open, and looks in a mirror

Mrs. Wilberforce is busying about downstairs. Marcus sings to himself

MARCUS   ...dididlididadada...

There is a board with sheets of music on it in one corner of the room

Marcus comes in, wiping his face with a towel and humming merrily to himself

He throws the towel onto the bed, opens a suitcase and takes something out—a wind-up gramophone

MARCUS (CONT'D)   Duddle-li-di-dum-dum-dum.

He places it on a table and takes a record out. He takes the disc from its sleeve and places it on the gramophone

He winds it, but doesn't play it

MARCUS (CONT'D)   ...dum-di-dum-di-dum.

He turns to the board, stops for a moment, and thinks

He walks up to the board and spins it around. On the other side is what looks like a complicated diagram, a map of some sort?

He stares at it for a second

MARCUS (CONT'D) Meh.

He spins it back around

MARCUS (CONT'D) It's the ending, Marcus, you don't have an ending. Never mind, never mind. It'll come. It always does.

Downstairs, the doorbell rings

SFX Doorbell

MARCUS (CONT'D) Oh! Mrs. Wilberforce?!

MARCUS springs to life. He dashes out to the landing while putting his jacket on, and sees her going for the door.

MARCUS (CONT'D) Eh, it's all right, Mrs. Wilberforce! It'll be my friends!

He swoops down the stairs, just getting in front of her, and opens the door to a man with a violin case

MARCUS (CONT'D) Ah! Good morning, Major Courtney!
MAJOR Ah! Yes! And to you, eh ...
MARCUS Professor.
MAJOR Professor! Professor Marcus. Yes, it is indeed a good evening. Why, why, why, such an evening...morning! Such a morning as has never been... been... eh... sorry... bit nervous...
MARCUS (*beaming at Mrs. W*) Calm down, Major. You're not a criminal and Mrs. Wilberforce here is not a... ha, ha... not a policeman!

Major Courtney visibly suffers at even the mention of the word

MRS. WILBERFORCE Major Courtney, hello.
MAJOR Hello. Ha, ha! A police... policeman! How...how amusing... the idea that a lady such as yourself could be among the ranks of the police really is very, very witty ha HA HA ha ha!

MARCUS Mrs. Wilberforce, the Major's nervous disposition is the unfortunate consequence of battle fatigue. We are in the presence of a war hero.

MAJOR Good heavens, are we?

MARCUS Yes, you.

MAJOR Oh, yes, of course!

MARCUS (CONT'D) I'm afraid his experiences during our finest hour have left him a shadow of his former self. A very brave man with all the appearance of an appalling idiot and coward.

MAJOR Ha, ha! Was that a — sorry, was that a joke? Ha, ha! What an amusing... or possibly very wise thing to say!

MARCUS Taken as a prisoner of war in 1940, the Major escaped five years later through sheer ingenuity and force of will.

MAJOR I dressed as a woman. I should add that it was an extremely common form of escape at the time. Everyone was doing it.

MARCUS If you don't mind, Mrs. Wilberforce, We must crack on.

MRS. WILBERFORCE Oh, yes, yes, of course. Professor Marcus told me all about your plans for the week!

MAJOR (*alarmed*) Good heavens, did he?

MARCUS The concert.

MAJOR Oh, yes! The, ah, yes... with the musical instruments and everything.

The doorbell rings again

SFX Doorbell

MARCUS I'll get it, Mrs. Wilberforce! Ha, ha!

MRS. WILBERFORCE May I ask where you were stationed during the war, Major Courtney?

Marcus pauses, waiting for the Major's answer

MAJOR I'm afraid that's still classified information.

MRS.WILBERFORCE Of course. "Loose lips".

Mrs. Wilberforce wanders away to meet the new arrival. The Major sees the parrot cage and lifts up the cover

MAJOR Ahh!

Marcus opens the door to reveal a cheerful-looking young spiv

HARRY Love the location, doc. Down at the end of lonely street, eh?

MARCUS Shh, get in. (*theatrically, whisking him in*) Well, Mister
Robinson! How are you? May I introduce Mister Robinson, Mrs.
Wilberforce?
HARRY Hello, dear! Call me 'Arry!
MARCUS Mister Robinson is one of our best loved—

The doorbell rings

SFX Doorbell

MARCUS (CONT'D) Excuse me.

He runs back to the door

*There is a huge man outside. An ex-boxer, he looks and sounds like he's
severely, permanently punch-drunk, and carries a cello case*

MARCUS (CONT'D) I thought I told you to stagger it!
ONE-ROUND I did stagger!
MRS. WILBERFORCE (*to Harry*) One of our best loved?...
HARRY (*totally lost*) Eh...
MARCUS (*from the door*) VIOLINISTS! ONE OF OUR BEST LOVED
VIOLINISTS!
HARRY (*holds up violin case*) That's right! I'm one of our best loved
violinists. Lovely place you have here, Mrs. Wilberforce! Is that an
original Constable I see?

He indicates a painting behind her

MRS. WILBERFORCE (*turns around*) What? Oh, no, no, my husband...
when he was alive, my husband used to love painting this particular
stretch of wood.

Harry takes the opportunity to slip a candlestick up one of his sleeves

She turns back around

MRS. WILBERFORCE (CONT'D) It's the view from the hill near
Wormwood Scrubs. Do you know it?
HARRY Very well.
GENERAL GORDON *You naughty boy!!*
HARRY What was that!?
MRS. WILBERFORCE General Gordon. Don't mind him, he's just
excited at all the commotion. Do you want to say hello?

She lifts the cover

Harry looks at it for a second

HARRY I still have no idea what that is.
MRS. WILBERFORCE He's a South American Macaw.
HARRY Which is a kind of?...
MRS. WILBERFORCE Parrot.
HARRY Parrot! Are you sure?
MRS. WILBERFORCE Oh, yes. I'm afraid he can be quite abrupt with new people.

Looking somewhat shaken, he reaches in his pockets, takes out some pills and pops one

MRS. WILBERFORCE (CONT'D) Oh, dear, you're not ill, are you, Mister Robinson?
HARRY Nah, they sort of wake me up. Keep me— you know. Gotta be— like that. So much going on sometimes... I wouldn't want to miss anything. (*looks at cage*) Except maybe... whatever that is.
MARCUS (*with One-Round, again with a flourish*) Mr.Lawson, Mrs. Wilberforce.
ONE-ROUND (*to Marcus*) Am I Mister Lawson?
MARCUS Ha, ha! "Am I Mister Lawson?" How marvellous! What a wonderful example of the eccentric and often confusing things you sometimes say!
MRS. WILBERFORCE Mister Lawson, a pleasure to meet you.
ONE-ROUND Hello, M'm.
MARCUS Where's your cello, Mister Lawson?
ONE-ROUND Who's Mister Lawson?
MARCUS (*sotto, furious*) Get your cello from the car! (*turning and beaming at Mrs. W*) What a massive talent! Sorry, you're, ah....

She is standing on his scarf again, again oblivious. He pulls it from under her foot, staggering back slightly

A dark shadow enters the doorway. This is Louis. He says nothing, instead pointing his violin case at Mrs. Wilberforce like a gun

MARCUS (CONT'D) (*sotto voce*) Get back! I told you to stagg— (*for Mrs. W's benefit*) Ahhh, what a coincidence that everyone's arriving at exactly the same time! Mister Harvey, this is Mrs. Wilberforce, who I told you about.

Louis gives her a single, curt nod. Then, he walks past her and starts casing the joint, covering the whole house in a matter of seconds

MARCUS (CONT'D) He's the temperamental one!
MRS. WILBERFORCE *(impressed)* Oooh!

LOUIS comes back down impatiently to see MARCUS ushering HARRY and MAJOR COURTNEY up the stairs. There is a kerfuffle mid-stairs with them all getting jammed together

MARCUS All right, everybody! Shall we begin? I apologise in advance for our fearsome scratchings, Mrs. Wilberforce!

SFX Doorbell

Marcus pushes Harry out of the way. Harry falls on his arse, and Marcus runs back down the stairs, once again just getting in front of Mrs. Wilberforce. He opens the door

ONE-ROUND *(brightly)* I'm Mister Lawson!
MARCUS Ha, ha! That's right, Mister Lawson, up the stairs with you!

He ushers all of them up the stairs and in to his rooms

MR. WILBERFORCE *(calling to them)* Perhaps, a cup of tea?...

UPSTAIRS...

MARCUS *(leaning out of his room's door)* Thank you all the same, Mrs. Wilberforce, but we must begin at once. But again thank you ever so much! Thank you, thank you, thank you.

He closes the door, and spins around to the room

HARRY What a delightful old person!
MARCUS Shh!

Marcus walks over to the GRAMOPHONE. He lifts the needle onto the record and Boccherini's minuet fills the air

SFX Boccherini

Marcus turns the trumpet part of the gramophone so that it is broadcasting directly below

DOWNSTAIRS...

Mrs. Wilberforce in her daily routine, has paused at the missing candlestick

Mrs. Wilberforce hears the music and suddenly stops in her tracks. She looks up at the ceiling, entranced. When she moves again, there is a certain lightness in her step. She's delighted

UPSTAIRS...

Marcus stands up from the gramophone, satisfied

MARCUS   It's not Doc this time. It's Professor. We're musicians, remember?

Harry shrugs and opens his case, and takes out a VIOLIN. One-Round opens his case and looks at the CELLO

ONE-ROUND   Oh! (*to Harry*) I've got a giant one!
LOUIS   I don't like it! I don't like her!
MARCUS   She's perfect, what are you talking about? Someone who wouldn't notice anything unusual! What is she if not that?
LOUIS   I don't like old ladies! They give me the penises.

Long pause as everyone takes this in

Harry bursts out laughing

HARRY   I'm sorry, I sort of told him that was the phrase. (*to Louis*) Willies.
LOUIS   What?
HARRY   Willies. They give you the willies. Oh, I do apologise. I never thought that would actually work.

He doubles over, laughing

LOUIS   I tell you I don't like it!
MARCUS   I'm not changing the plan, Louis, not at this late stage.
LOUIS   You haven't even told us the plan.
MARCUS   That's WHY we're HERE!

He spins the BLACKBOARD around, revealing the PLAN

MAJOR Good gracious. There it is, what? We're really doing it. Oh, dear. Marcus, where's the best place to...?

Marcus points to the window and Major Courtney puts his head through the curtains. A retching sound. He pulls his head back in, wiping his mouth with his sleeve

MAJOR (CONT'D) Don't worry. Got it on the tracks.
HARRY Thanks for the picture.

He offers the Major a pill

HARRY (CONT'D) Here. Have a blue one. (*shrugs*) I use them to calm down after a red one.
MAJOR Thank you, Harry.
HARRY (*takes another bottle out*) You'll need one of these yellows in about five minutes.
LOUIS (*looking at plan*)A decoy car. Yes, yes, clever. I'll need to set off first, though. Give me a pen.
MARCUS Leave it alone! Get away from the plan, get away!

He shoos Louis away

MARCUS (CONT'D) (*composing himself*) There's still work to do anyway.
LOUIS What work?
MARCUS The ending lacks... I don't know. Finesse.
ONE-ROUND What's finesse?
MARCUS Polish, One-Round.
ONE-ROUND Place looks all right to me.
MARCUS ...refinement, delicacy, grace...
LOUIS It's a stick up job, not the Sistine Chapel!
HARRY Let him do his thing, will you, Louis? Always worked for us before.
MAJOR I think you'll find Marcus is very capable.
HARRY He's the best.
LOUIS So you keep saying.
MAJOR In those of the Professor's manoeuvres in which I have participated, there has never been a hitch.
LOUIS Then why are you a nervous ship?
MARCUS Wreck. Nervous wreck, Louis. Your command of English is very impressive but I'd stay away from the whole area of idioms.
LOUIS Whatever! He's all over the place!

MAJOR It was that thing in the cage. It gave me a terrible turn.

HARRY It's a parrot.

MAJOR That was a *parrot*? I've never seen anything like it. It looks like a starving baby in a sock.

MARCUS Be assured, Louis, Major Courtney is one of our finest confidence men, despite his lack of confidence as a man. Now, gentlemen, on one matter, my Rumanian friend and I are in complete agreement. We must bring clarity of thought to the matter in hand. That security van is not going to rob itself. No! It needs our *assistance*!

There is a KNOCK AT THE DOOR...

MARCUS (CONT'D) Quick! Into position!

Marcus spins the blueprint around and it whaps Harry under the chin

HARRY OW! Bloody Nora!

The men grab their instruments and stand behind their music stands

One-Round lifts the cello to his chin. Marcus takes it off him and shoves it between One-Round's legs

Professor Marcus turns the record off, and swings open the door to reveal the musicians, standing at their posts

MRS. WILBERFORCE You have been dishonest with me, Professor!

MARCUS What?

MRS. WILBERFORCE All of you have! You're not amateur musicians!

The Major makes a strangled noise

MRS. WILBERFORCE (CONT'D) You *must* be professionals! You're every bit as good!

The Major exhales with relief, noisily

MARCUS Oh, not quite! But we are rather proud of Mister Harvey's timbre.

MRS. WILBERFORCE (*to One-Round*) ...and that pizzicato passage, Mr. Lawson. Exquisite! How do you do it with such huge hands?

One-Round looks at his hands, suddenly amazed at his own powers

ONE-ROUND I don't know!

MRS. WILBERFORCE You were all wonderful, quite wonderful.

MAJOR (*honestly flattered*) Thank you very much, ma'am.

MRS. WILBERFORCE You know, I was so surprised when I heard what you were playing. It brought back something that really I'd forgotten all about. My twenty-first birthday party.

The men are listening to her now

MRS. WILBERFORCE (CONT'D) You see, my father had engaged a string quartet to come in and play in the evening. And while they were doing that same Boccherini piece, someone came in and said that the Old Queen had passed away.

(*beat*)

And that was the end of my party.

(*beat*)

All that time ago. In Pangbourne.

(*beat*)

I wonder, would you play it for me now? It would mean so much to me.

ONE-ROUND We'd love to!

MARCUS Ha, ha, yes, we'd love to, Mrs. Wilberforce. But we can't.

MRS. WILBERFORCE Oh!

ONE-ROUND Why not?

MRS. WILBERFORCE Well, perhaps tomorrow then?

ONE-ROUND We'd love to!

MARCUS Mister Lawson!! Ha, ha! You know perfectly well that tomorrow we will be preparing the second movement! Your fingers simply couldn't take the strain! Let alone your mental faculties!

One-Round looks at his hands again

ONE-ROUND Ohhh....yeah...

MARCUS I'm sorry, Mrs. Wilberforce, we simply can't do private performances until we are fully rehearsed. Though of course by the end of the week, we shall be very happy to perform for you.

He tries to usher her out

MRS. WILBERFORCE Oh! Thank you! Perhaps I might prepare some tea for you to express my—

MARCUS No need Mrs. Wilberforce! A good deed etcetera etcetera. Now, it really is crucial that we not be disturbed for the remainder of the day. Thank you so much, goodbye, goodbye.

He ushers her out

LOUIS Oh, don't send her away! Maybe she'll tell us another brilliant story!
MARCUS Just think of her as a silent partner. A very chatty silent partner.
LOUIS I tell you I don't like old ladies!

The men laugh

ONE-ROUND What are you scared of a little old lady for?

Louis takes out a knife and starts cleaning his fingernails with it

HARRY She might come at him with a poison biscuit.
LOUIS You know...I actually lost a knife inside the last person who laughed at me.

Harry stops laughing

LOUIS (CONT'D) Not this knife, obviously. A different knife.
MARCUS Gentlemen, gentlemen! Have we already forgotten why we are here?

He swings the blackboard around to reveal the plan, again clocking Harry on the head

A respectful silence descends

Marcus observes them for a moment

He taps the blackboard

MARCUS (CONT'D) This is the one. This is the one they'll remember me for. Isn't it lovely?
HARRY What's your timing on it?
MARCUS 11 minutes from top to toe, but I think we can bring it down to eight. Minimal level of violence— sorry, Louis— and the money... oh, the money. Close your eyes, gentlemen, and imagine what two hundred thousand pounds looks like. Imagine it floating down around you like snow. Imagine the sound as it riffles through your fingers...

There is a knock on the door as Mrs. Wilberforce arrives back at it

MARCUS (CONT'D) ...imagine...

The knocking continues. Marcus slumps slightly

One by one the men open their eyes and look at the door

The knocking continues

Louis, frustrated, throws his knife into the floor, where it glitters menacingly

The knocking continues, and then merges into the sound of the approaching train

The rumbling sound grows and then the train passes by, throwing the stage into darkness

SFX Whistle

UPSTAIRS...

Morning light. The men are all in shirtsleeves in Marcus's rooms, waiting. The Major is looking nervously out of the window. Harry is obsessively cleaning a spot on his violin. Louis is smoothing his hair, and One-Round is tunelessly playing around with the cello

ONE-ROUND It makes different sounds if you move your fingers. Look!

He scratches the cello tunelessly to demonstrate

Louis gives him a withering look, and then places his hat over his eyes, blocking everyone out. He puts his feet up and tries to get comfortable

In the sudden silence, we can hear the the noise of Harry obsessively cleaning a spot on his violin

Louis raises his hat

LOUIS Harry?
HARRY Yeah?
LOUIS What are you doing?
HARRY Bit of a mark. Just trying to...doesn't seem to want to come off.

Harry goes back to madly cleaning the violin

MAJOR   Good morning's work that. Better than yesterday. And yesterday was better than the day before that. Terrific stuff!
LOUIS   Pfft! There's no ending. None of it's worth a damn without the ending.

He's distracted by Harry's cleaning, which is becoming more intense

MAJOR   But he's on top of it, Louis. You'll see. Man's a genius. His mind... He'll come up with something extraordinary... That's how he works. Keeps you guessing till the last minute but always comes through in the end.
LOUIS   (*suddenly*) THERE'S NO MARK!
HARRY   What?
LOUIS   Stop bloody cleaning!

Harry stops cleaning

Frustrated at not being able to sleep, LOUIS swings to a seated position and accidentally kicks the record player

The needle bounces onto the disc, SCRATCHES painfully across it, and the music starts playing

Louis dives to the record player and picks up the needle

DOWNSTAIRS...

Mrs Wilberforce is on the phone. She stares up at the ceiling

MRS. WILBERFORCE   Sorry, Margaret, I'm still here. Yes, yes, a concert. The Professor said he'd— yes, they're wonderful. Perfectionists. They've been working on the same piece all week and they're getting awfully good.

Suddenly, Marcus bursts out of the upstairs toilet

MARCUS   I've got it! Oh! Excuse me, Mrs. Wilberforce.

He walks across the landing to the upstairs room, then remembers something and dashes back to the toilet for his notebook

MRS. WILBERFORCE Yes, we'll need refreshments! But tell the others to co-ordinate this time. We want to make sure we don't end up with a lot of fruitcakes. I am not whispering! Oh, goodbye, Margaret.

Now carrying the notebook, Marcus rushes back to the upstairs room

She puts the phone down and checks to make sure Marcus didn't hear

She goes to the kitchen and starts preparing some tea

Marcus bursts into the upstairs room

MARCUS I've got it!
LOUIS What have you got?
MARCUS The ending! The ending, Louis!
MAJOR You see? Genius!
LOUIS He hasn't told us it yet. Come on then, spill it on us. We are all of us ears.
MARCUS Could I ask you all to take your positions?

They all do so

ONE-ROUND What's the hatstand again?
MARCUS (*taking the record off again*) For the last time, the hatstand is a telephone box. Those chairs are the security van, and that chair is our truck. OK, now...
MAJOR Before we begin—
MARCUS What?!
MAJOR No, very simple question. Just wondering if it's absolutely necessary for me to be out in the field, as it were? Only, I always felt my strengths lay more in the field of—
MARCUS Major, you loiter inconspicuously looking like an insurance broker. Then you make a single phone-call. Were you any less involved in this robbery you would be working for the police.
MAJOR Yes, sorry, and it's after I see Harry dressed as the porter that I make my call. Ehm, 'The eagle has arrived at the nest!' Hello? Hello?
MARCUS Press button A, Major.
MAJOR Oh! Of course!

He presses an imaginary A button

MAJOR (CONT'D) The eagle has arrived at the nest.

MARCUS Thank you, Major.
HARRY Is this chair still the van then?

Louis hits him with a newspaper

HARRY (CONT'D) What's that all about?
LOUIS I give the van driver a sock. It's the plan!
HARRY That wouldn't knock anyone out.

Louis really socks him one

HARRY (CONT'D) Arrrgh! Take it easy!
LOUIS Will you go down before I use my real one?
HARRY Oh!

He remembers his role and falls down onto the floor

LOUIS Is this the money?

He holds up a lacy pillow. Marcus nods and grabs it

*Louis and Marcus transfer the money to the truck. They pretend to have
real trouble with it, like it's a heavy trunk*

Louis pretends to drive the 'van' away

LOUIS (CONT'D) Brum, brum, brum.

Harry jumps up from his position and becomes a railway porter

One-Round walks past him, moving his arms like a train

ONE-ROUND Chooo, choooo!
HARRY They know I'm a porter, you don't have to do the train!
MARCUS Oh, let him do the train.

*Louis puts the pillow on a chair Harry is using to represent a trolley.
Harry brings it to the 'station'*

They leave it standing in the middle of the room

LOUIS Right.
MARCUS Right.

LOUIS That's where we were! I don't understand! We get it to the station, but there'll be cops all over the place. How do we get it past the cops? Isn't that what the?...

MARCUS Gentlemen, could you take your places, please?

They go back to first positions

MARCUS (CONT'D) No, no, your places in the musical group.

LOUIS Why?

MARCUS Come in, Mrs. Wilberforce!

There is a pause, then a confused knock on the door

Marcus crosses to it

MARCUS (CONT'D) Haven't you noticed? She's through that door every fifteen minutes. It's like having a geriatric cuckoo clock.

Marcus swings the door open to reveal her standing there with all the tea things

MARCUS (CONT'D) Ah! Tea! Just what we were after! Thank you, Mrs. Wilberforce.

MRS. WILBERFORCE Oh, yes, I wondered whether you and the gentlemen would like... oh...

MARCUS Splendid, splendid! And while you're here, perhaps I could ask a favour? (*he picks up the pillow*) I was wondering if I could entreat you to bring this downstairs? I only need one pillow and I'm worried this one will get dusty.

MRS. WILBERFORCE Oh... yes, of course.

MARCUS Thank you so much, Mrs. Wilberforce. Goodbye! Goodbye!

She takes the pillow and he ushers her out

He turns and gives the men a significant look

HARRY Cor!

MAJOR That's brilliant!

LOUIS You're insane!

One-Round feels a pressure to say something...

ONE-ROUND I don't... I don't get it.

MARCUS They're looking for four men and not half an hour has passed since the robbery began. We just wind her up... and she brings. Us. The Money.

They all think about it for a second

MAJOR   The police will never stop her. This is your masterpiece, Marcus!

MARCUS Well, that's for others to say, not me. But I concur.

HARRY It's the dodgiest part of the job and we're not doing it!

LOUIS It's clever. I'll give you that. But I still don't like it. You can't work with anyone whose first priority is finding the nearest lavatory.

MARCUS Louis...

LOUIS I tell you I don't like old ladies! My mother sent me to live with one before the war. She smelled like a chimney. She had hair everywhere. From the stuff in her ears alone you could have made a broom! She used to...pull me onto her lap and tell me fairy stories... (*he shivers*) ...I tell you I was less afraid of the Germans!

MARCUS Well, one bad apple. No, I've looked at this from every angle and there is no way any of us can get the money back from St Pancras. And I trust we are all agreed as to the centrality of the money in our little scheme? Hmm?

HARRY Well, I'm in.

MAJOR You know me, Marcus. I'm right behind you.

MARCUS Louis? I think you'll find that far from being a weak link, Mrs. Wilberforce is our salvation.

Pause

LOUIS I don't like it. But I'm in.

There is a knock on the door

Marcus wasn't expecting this

MARCUS Eh...yes?

The door opens, and Mrs. Wilberforce is standing there, an unhappy smile on her face

MRS. WILBERFORCE Professor, I've... I've... Oh, dear!

MARCUS   Harry, move out of the way, One-Round, help Mrs. Wilberforce to a chair. Major, get some water. Louis...

Louis is standing nearby with a very uncomfortable look on his face

MARCUS (CONT'D) ...never mind.

The men go about their tasks, but Mrs. Wilberforce's distress has an unhappy effect on them. Uncoordinated and taken by surprise by their new roles, they smack into each other, trip over items from the robbery etc. etc. Harry even manages to get hit by the blackboard again

HARRY Owwwwww!!...
MRS. WILBERFORCE Oh, professor, I've done a terrible thing! A terrible thing!
MARCUS Why Mrs. Wilberforce! Whatever is the matter?
MRS. WILBERFORCE Oh, it's dreadful, it's quite dreadful!

They gather around her to listen

HARRY *(under his breath)* This'll be good.
MARCUS What is it, Mrs. Wilberforce?

She is treading on his scarf again. He tries to pull it loose, she steps toward a chair, and releases it, and Marcus staggers back slightly.

MRS. WILBERFORCE I am a member of a loose society of elderly women.
HARRY *(under his breath)* Already brilliant.
MRS. WILBERFORCE *(sitting)* We gather at one another's homes for the purpose of presenting some form of cultural event. The last time I hosted, everyone seemed very moved by my reading of my late husband's logbook. My husband, Arthur, kept very detailed logs while in the Navy...
HARRY Well, it's the food, isn't it?

Marcus throws him a disgusted look

MRS. WILBERFORCE ...everyone said they greatly enjoyed the evening. But they haven't been back since. They keep *skipping* me. I thought I might win them back with something they could not ignore so I told them...oh, dear.... I told them all that you'd do a concert, a performance. For our society!
MARCUS Ah.
MRS. WILBERFORCE Oh, I feel terrible. Terrible!
MARCUS Now, now Mrs. Wilberforce. There's really no need for this. When was this concert due to take place?

MRS. WILBERFORCE Next Friday, teatime.

MARCUS Well, it was rather naughty of you not to consult us, but of course we should be delighted to play for you and your friends.

HARRY Wha—?

Louis hits him to shut him up

MARCUS No, we'd love to, wouldn't we everyone?

The 'band' all look at each other

ALL .... we'd be delighted... yeah... all right... suppose so... great chance to perform.

ONE-ROUND Isn't there some reason we can't??

MARCUS No, Mr. Lawson...

ONE-ROUND I'm sure there is.

MARCUS *SHUT* ...that door over there, would you, One-Round?

One-Round, confused, goes to the door and shuts it

MARCUS (CONT'D) Mrs. Wilberforce, we'd be delighted. I do however have a tiny favour to ask of you in return. A package I need met at the station.

MRS. WILBERFORCE Oh, yes! Anything!

MARCUS Wonderful!

MRS. WILBERFORCE Thank you, Professor! Thank you, gentlemen!

MARCUS Dry those eyes, Mrs. Wilberforce!

MRS. WILBERFORCE I can't tell you how delighted I am! I'll get my yellow dress out! With you playing the Boccherini, it will be just like my 21st Birthday all over again!

She leaves

MARCUS (*to the others*) We'll be long gone.

MAJOR (*to Louis*) You see? His mind!

ONE-ROUND What, we're not really giving a concert?

MARCUS Of course not!

ONE-ROUND Oh.

He doesn't look happy. Marcus turns with a tray. There are some glasses on it and a bottle of wine. He offers them to the men, who take a glass each

MARCUS Gentlemen, a fine week's work. All that remains is the trivial
matter of the robbery itself. May I ask you to raise your glasses?

They do so

MARCUS (CONT'D) Mozart, Van Gogh, Cezanne, Rembrandt. Can
you tell me what they all have in common? (*pause*) They all died poor.
Well, bugger that.

Everyone except Louis laughs and drinks. One-nil to Marcus

Pause

LOUIS Hm.
MARCUS (*exasperated*) Oh! What is it now?
LOUIS Well... I notice she didn't actually take the pillow.

*The men turn and stare at the pillow, which is indeed still in the middle
of the room*

THE MUSIC SWELLS, AND MIXES TO...

*...THE SOUNDS OF CAR TYRES SCREECHING, A YELL, A POLICE
WHISTLE...*

...THE SOUNDS OF KINGS CROSS...

....THE WHISTLING AND SCREECHING OF STEAM TRAINS...

*AND THE MUSIC BRINGS US BACK TO MRS. WILBERFORCE'S
SITTING-ROOM...*

A floral, frilly dress hangs in view...

Harry comes through the front door

HARRY Hello? Hello?

He checks his watch

HARRY (CONT'D) They should be back. They should be well back.

He goes to the window and looks outside

HARRY (CONT'D) All right, take it easy, take it easy.

He pops open his pill-bottle and is about to swallow one when—

GENERAL GORDON *Squawk!!*

The pill hops out of his hand and drops onto the floor

GENERAL GORDON (CONT'D) Stay for tea! Squawk! Please stay
   for tea!
HARRY Gah! Bloody bugger!

*Harry looks around for the pill, a search that takes him over to where
Louis has been hiding (!)*

In an instant, Louis has his knife at Harry's neck

HARRY (CONT'D) Jesus!
LOUIS You took your time!
HARRY What are you talking about?
LOUIS You were supposed to be back before me!
HARRY Bollocks I was! I had to finish my shift, didn't I? How would
   it look if I just took off?
LOUIS Did it work?
HARRY What?
LOUIS Was Mrs. Wilberforce at the station?
HARRY Yes. No. I don't know! I just dropped the trunk off where I
   was told.

Louis lets him go

LOUIS I don't like this.
HARRY *You* don't like this. I'm bleeding! What was all that about?
LOUIS I won't be happy until Marcus *and* the money are through that
   door.

SFX Doorbell

LOUIS (CONT'D) Hide!

They run up to the Professor's rooms...

DOWNSTAIRS...

The Major opens the front door. He is dressed as a city gent

MAJOR Hello? Hello?

He checks his watch

MAJOR (CONT'D) Funny. Sure Louis was supposed to be back first...

He sees the pretty, frilly dress hanging up. He looks around

He crosses to the dress

He has another look around before...

...he takes the dress, lifts it to his chin and starts to sway, visibly relaxing

Louis and Harry have slipped out of the Professor's rooms, and are standing watching at the TOP OF THE STAIRS

MAJOR (CONT'D) (*sings the Boccherini piece*) Yada liddle lum, dum, dum, dum...

He mumbles to himself

MAJOR (CONT'D) Oh, yes!... most beautiful woman in the world! Who wants to marry me? Everyone! Ha, ha, ha! Well, you can't! Because I'm unattainable!
LOUIS What the hell are you doing?
MAJOR AHHHHH!
LOUIS What were you doing with that dress?
MAJOR I was...I was...I resent the...I was merely...how dare you, sir! How dare you! I was merely... I merely fell against the dress while singing!
LOUIS What is going on? Is this something to do with Mrs. Wilberforce? Is this the plan?
MAJOR No, no, I'm just... I'm just an admirer of the cut. I used to know a seamstress!
LOUIS Sit down! Both of you!
HARRY You "fell against the dress".
LOUIS Shut up! Something is going on and I have to think! I have to think!

He takes the knife out and starts playing with it. Harry moves away from him quickly

MAJOR What's going on? Everything's still working, isn't it? Nothing's going wrong!

LOUIS Where's Marcus!? He should have been back before any of us! And where's the old lady? I tell you what's happening, she's in on it!

HARRY What? Oh, you're silly in the head, you are!

MAJOR Absolute poppycock! Mrs. Wilberforce is the very soul of decency!

LOUIS Something's going on, I tell you!

HARRY (*checks watch*) Well... One-Round is a bit late...

LOUIS (*snaps fingers*) That's it! He's double-crossing us, but he's using One-Round as protection! It's a two-way split!

One-Round's shadow falls against the door

LOUIS (CONT'D) It's One-Round! Hide!

They start to hide

MAJOR Why are we hiding! Everything is working! This is still the plan!!

One-Round tries the door: locked

ONE-ROUND Hello? (*shouts*) Hello? HELLO! Is anyone back from THE ROBBERY!?

LOUIS Open the door, open the door!

Harry runs to the door. He opens it to reveal One-Round dressed in his usual fashion

HARRY Will you shut up, you great pillock!

ONE-ROUND What? (*realises*) Oh, yeah. "Hello, I'm Mr. Lawson."

LOUIS Oh, shut up!

ONE-ROUND What's wrong with everyone?

HARRY Ohhhhh, shit! Ohhhhhhh!

LOUIS What? What is it?

HARRY What? Oh, sorry, no, it's just... kicking in. Bloody hell. I tell you, these red ones.

He looks around

HARRY (CONT'D) Look at the state of this place!

Harry starts cleaning

MAJOR Don't worry about it, One-Round. They've worked themselves into a lather over nothing.

ONE-ROUND That's a nice dress.

MAJOR Shut up about the dress!

LOUIS We're trying to figure out if we've been double-crossed! Something is going on!

MAJOR Oh, nothing is going on!

LOUIS Then where is Marcus? *Where is he?!*

Suddenly, we hear the W.C. flush

Everyone freezes. Even Harry stops his cleaning

A door at the side of the stage swings open—a previously unseen downstairs loo—and Marcus emerges

MARCUS (*cool as you like*) Well...I brought the newspaper in to read but I really shouldn't have bothered. That was enough entertainment for a week... (*to Harry*) You missed a spot.

Harry looks and starts cleaning again

Marcus picks up MRS.WILBERFORCE'S dress

LOUIS How long have you been back?

MARCUS (*pointedly, to the Major*) I'll put this away, shall I, Major? I understand you fell against it.

LOUIS How long have you been back, I said!

MARCUS Do you want the paper? I've had about all I can stand of our little adventure in the Middle East.

He walks past them and up the stairs. They stand there, stunned

ONE-ROUND Wasn't that him?

Louis runs to the foot of the stairs

LOUIS Hey! Where's the money?

MARCUS (*sitting in his room, reading, shouting back*) It's coming, Louis! How poor are they, that have not patience! By the way, what was the point of hitting the van driver after he was unconscious?

LOUIS You look after your own business.

MARCUS It is my business! We kill anyone it's that much harder to get away!

LOUIS Pfft. Where's the old lady?

MARCUS Oh, Louis, have confidence in the steady ship that is Mrs.
    Wilberforce. She should be toodling into sight round about— rum
    pum diddlee um dum dum— now.

One-Round is at the window

ONE-ROUND It's Mrs. Wilberforce!

MARCUS There!

Harry makes a frightened sound

MARCUS (CONT'D) What's wrong with you?

HARRY It's the filth!

MAJOR Oh, Harry, the place looks fine.

HARRY No, no, she's got the filth with her! A rozzer!

The Major looks quite faint. Even Marcus reels as if from a blow

MARCUS But...but that's not part of the plan!

Cornered, they look around desperately

HARRY (*tugging uniform*) If anyone sees me in this!

For a few moments, chaos reigns as they they look for an escape route

*Then, Marcus runs, swings open the door to a TINY CUPBOARD, and
urges them all inside. We see a NAVY UNIFORM and some other clothes
in there*

Finally, the gang are all in and the door swings shut

*Mrs. Wilberforce and Constable MacDonald open the front door. The
latter carrying a LARGE, HEAVY TRUNK*

CONSTABLE MACDONALD Musicians, you say?

MRS. WILBERFORCE Yes. A chamber quintet.

CONSTABLE MACDONALD Have to say, I'd never be a musician,
    Mrs. Wilberforce.

MRS. WILBERFORCE No? Why is that, Constable?

He plomps down the trunk and then leans on it

CONSTABLE MACDONALD No money in it.

MRS. WILBERFORCE Oh, they're not in it for the money, Constable.
 They do it for love. They are artists, of the most noble stripe. God's
 instruments.

CONSTABLE MACDONALD Oh, lovely.

MRS. WILBERFORCE Are you going? I'm sure they'd like to thank
 you for your help.

CONSTABLE MACDONALD No, I'd imagine a policeman is the last
 person they'd want to speak to. Where shall I put the, ah...

MRS. WILBERFORCE Oh, in the cupboard, thank you.

CONSTABLE MACDONALD Yes, wouldn't want to miss out on the
 fun if we actually manage to catch the buggers. Oh, beg your pardon,
 Mrs. Wilberforce.

MRS. WILBERFORCE No, no, my husband was in the navy.

CONSTABLE MACDONALD Though with my luck, the men we're
 looking for are probably miles away by now.

*MRS WILBERFORCE swings the door of the small cupboard open
revealing the men sitting inside*

MARCUS Hello!

The men all join in with a friendly wave

MRS. WILBERFORCE Good heavens! Whatever are you all doing in
 there, Professor?

MARCUS What are we doing in here?

MRS. WILBERFORCE Yes!

Pause

MARCUS Oh, WHAT are we doing?

MRS. WILBERFORCE Yes.

MARCUS Oh, I misheard you! Ehm, well, we're discussing
 something.

Pause

MRS. WILBERFORCE Oh...what are you discussing?

MARCUS 'What' are we discussing? Wh-well... we're discussing...
 we're discussing...

He's thoroughly rattled. Pause

None of the men know what to say

Finally, One-Round opens his mouth

ONE-ROUND The pissycat's passage?
MARCUS   The pizzicato passage! Yes, One-Round— MISTER
    LAWSON feels it's too slow, and my companions and I were trying to
    persuade him otherwise. It's not too slow, Mister Lawson!

Everyone in the cupboard joins in trying to reassure Mr.Lawson

MRS. WILBERFORCE But why are you discussing it... in there?

All the men look at each other

MARCUS Why? Ha, ha, ha! Mrs. Wilberforce... we are artists!
MRS. WILBERFORCE Oh. Yes. Yes, of course! I do apologise.
MARCUS Would you mind?

She closes the door and turns to Constable MacDonald

MARCUS (CONT'D) (*from inside*) Mister Lawson, please! Enough
    nonsense, you are the finest cellist I have ever worked with, and were
    the passage too slow, I would be the first to tell you. Or do you doubt
    my judgement as a conductor?

Pause

MARCUS (CONT'D) Well?

Pause

ONE-ROUND Am I Mister L—
MARCUS Then it's settled! So, shall we... Shall we, ah...Shall we go
    back in? Yes, yes... ah... any other business? Yes, then... let's... wander
    back in and... and say hello to... to, eh... our, eh...

He opens the door and affects delight to see the pair

MARCUS (CONT'D) ...Mrs. Wilberforce, how wonderful to see you!

*The rest, save Harry, come out as Marcus pretends to notice the
policeman*

MARCUS (CONT'D) And who is this proud member of her Majesty's greatest servant, the police force?

Louis quietly shuts the door of the cupboard as he leaves

MRS. WILBERFORCE Oh! This is Constable MacDonald!

MARCUS A Scot! The finest race!

CONSTABLE MACDONALD I'm not Scottish.

MARCUS Even better! (*under his breath, to Louis*) Oh, Mister Harvey, I meant to say, we might have to take out that troublesome passage. You know the one.

LOUIS You know, I have been thinking the same thing.

MARCUS Yes, a straightforward cut.

LOUIS Let me find my score.

He moves to position himself behind the Constable

MRS. WILBERFORCE Professor Marcus, have you heard? There's been a robbery!

MAJOR Ngyahhhaaaaa...

MRS. WILBERFORCE (*to the Major*) Yes, isn't it terrible?

MARCUS Really?

CONSTABLE MACDONALD Security van. Very vicious operation. The driver... well, it's not looking good.

MARCUS & MRS.WILBERFORCE How awful.

CONSTABLE MACDONALD We only have one thing to go on. we believe they may be trying to take the money out by rail. So one of them is possibly disguised as some sort of railway employee.

MRS. WILBERFORCE Where's Mister Robinson?

MAJOR Ngyahahaaaa....

Pause

MRS. WILBERFORCE He's not here.

MARCUS Let's see...one, two, three, four...you're right. He may be having a sleep upstairs.

MRS. WILBERFORCE But he was in there. With you. He's...

She turns to the closet

MRS. WILBERFORCE (CONT'D) ...he's *still* in there.

They all look at the door

MRS. WILBERFORCE (CONT'D) He's still *in* there.

MARCUS Is he? Let me just have a check. (*knocks on the door*) Mister Robinson?

Pause

HARRY Yes?

MARCUS (*to Mrs. Wilberforce*) By heavens, you were right!

(*to closet*) Mr. Robinson, you are in there!

HARRY Yes, I'm...I'm in here, all right!

MARCUS Well, that's sorted out then. You were right he is still in there.

MRS. WILBERFORCE But *why* is he still in there?

MARCUS Good question. Why are you still in there, Mister Robinson?

HARRY The lack of air... made me confused... and I got lost.

MARCUS Lost in such a small space! Why, you must have been confused indeed!

The Constable moves to allow Louis to get behind him. Louis immediately slows, turns, and starts to creep back towards the policeman

CONSTABLE MACDONALD Aren't you going to come out, sir?

HARRY The door's jammed.

MARCUS D'ya know what, he's right, it won't budge.

ONE-ROUND I'll have a go.

MARCUS Mister Lawson! Mister Lawson, no—

ONE-ROUND Maybe there's a trick to it.

He swings his big meaty fist at the door and it CRASHES open...

...revealing HARRY, wearing a patterned V-neck sweater over a shirt and tie and tan corduroy slacks. If it weren't for the fact that the clothes are slightly too big for him, he would look like the perfect 1940s family man

Pause

MARCUS Harry, Constable MacDonald.

MRS. WILBERFORCE Oh, Mister Robinson! For a moment there you were the very image of my late husband.

HARRY I've that sort of face.

MARCUS Allow me to see you out, Constable. You'd better get back on the trail of those awful, awful men. Gentlemen?

The men grab the trunk and immediately start lugging it upstairs

CONSTABLE MACDONALD I wouldn't worry, Professor... King's Cross is sewn up! Nothing's getting out of there! I think those Gentlemen may have bitten off more than they can chew when they tangled with us.
MARCUS Yes, I wouldn't like to be in their shoes.

He leads him outside and slams the door shut with his foot

MARCUS turns and makes for the stairs

MARCUS (CONT'D) Some tea, perhaps, Mrs. Wilberforce!
MRS. WILBERFORCE (*hasn't even got her coat off*) Oh! How rude of me! Yes, I...yes...

Marcus gets into the upstairs room just as ONE-ROUND pops open the trunk to reveal the money. A very impressive sight

ONE-ROUND Cor. Look at that.

Pause

MARCUS (*to Louis*) And now, with the police surrounding the station, we simply drive away. I found my ending. A masterpiece.
HARRY (*jumpy still*) I need a wee.
MARCUS (*while slapping the prone Major round the face*) Your first as a rich man! Enjoy it, Harry!
LOUIS The job isn't over until we're out of London.
MARCUS A few loose ends, Louis, that's all. Could you do a quick sweep for fingerprints? Best to be on the safe side.
MAJOR Of course.
MARCUS Louis, start the car. One-Round, get our things. I shall take a few moments of mental respite.

He sits in a chair and looks 'artistic'. Basically his way of avoiding work

Meanwhile, around him, a hive of activity

Louis runs out to the car. One-Round starts collecting the cases. The Major quickly revives and starts to rub every single surface he and the others have touched during their stay with a cloth

Harry comes out from his toilet break and sees the Major. He starts following the Major around and cleaning everything that the Major has already done, evidently unhappy with the job he's doing

Upstairs, One-Round sits on the trunk. He is about to put the cello away when he stops for a moment, then picks it up. He takes the bow and plays the first few notes of the minuet again

Tuneless though it is, he actually manages to hit the first few notes, but the fourth one is hopelessly off

One-Round stops, sighs, and puts the cello down

The Major stops cleaning

MAJOR That's everything.
HARRY Not quite.

Two candlesticks slide down his sleeves and into his hands

The Major gives him a disapproving look

Harry gives them both an extra special clean and places them back on the mantelpiece

All the men are now gathered again in the sitting-room

MARCUS Good job, everyone! I'll just let Mrs. Wilberforce know we're off. You know in a funny old way I'm going to miss the old—

They all freeze as Mrs. Wilberforce steps out on to the landing, resplendent in her dress

Pause

ONE-ROUND You look well nice, m'm.
MRS. WILBERFORCE Thank you, Mr Lawson.
MARCUS Ah! A vision! An angel!
MRS. WILBERFORCE Professor, I was wondering if I might ask one question about the concert?

She comes downstairs as she speaks

MARCUS The concert.

MRS. WILBERFORCE Yes, would your companions be amenable to a brief question and answer session following the performance?

MARCUS Oh, yes, yes, next week's concert.

MRS. WILBERFORCE Today's concert.

MARCUS Next Friday, we said, yes?

MRS. WILBERFORCE Friday, today.

Marcus looks panicked suddenly

MARCUS No, no, next Friday means Friday week. If I'd meant today I would have just said "Friday". "Next Friday" suggests the Friday following this Friday.

MRS. WILBERFORCE No, next Friday means the Friday that is next!

HARRY That's what I thought you meant.

MARCUS No, are you—this is why you're dressed up! (*to the men*) Hurry up! We need to get out of here! (*to Mrs. Wilberforce*) Mrs. Wilberforce, I do apologise but we are unable to do the concert.

MRS. WILBERFORCE Wh...what?

MARCUS I'm afraid there really is nothing we can do. The entire string section of the Prague Philarmonic has caught the Irish mumps. It's a very rare disease of the inner elbow. They need replacements quickly and it's an opportunity I really can't deny my companions.

MRS. WILBERFORCE Oh... well... I do understand, I suppose... oh, dear...

They gather all their things to leave

ONE-ROUND (*leaving*) Goodbye, Mrs. Wilberforce!

HARRY The case, brains!

ONE-ROUND Oh, the... oh, yeah!

One-Round comes back and picks the huge trunk up. Mrs. Wilberforce goes up to the Professor, stepping on his scarf again

MRS. WILBERFORCE Professor, whatever shall I tell my friends?

MARCUS Oh, I'm sure they'll be as delighted with your company as we were.

He jerks his scarf from under her foot again, nearly falling over

MARCUS Anyway, off we go! Thanks again, Mrs. Wilberforce, we shall be forever in your debt!

He adjusts the picture again as he passes it

The men line up in front of her

One-Round is at the end of the queue

The Major steps forward and removes his hat

MAJOR It has been... an honour.
MRS. WILBERFORCE Thank you, Major. I can't tell you what it has
    meant having a military man in this house once again.

*This catches the Major by surprise. He opens his mouth to respond, but
then finally just bows and leaves*

Harry approaches

MRS. WILBERFORCE (CONT'D) Thank you again, Mr. Robinson,
    for the music and for all your work during the week. The house has
    never looked lovelier.
HARRY Nah, nah, don't mention it, I enjoyed it! Goodbye, dear!

Harry leaves and the line moves forward again

*Louis is next. He seems unsure as to what to do. Finally, he reaches out
and gives her an odd little pat on the head*

LOUIS Goodbye, old woman.
MRS.WILBERFORCE Oh. Yes. Goodbye.

Louis leaves

MRS. WILBERFORCE Mister Lawson, I shall miss your cello playing
    most of all.
ONE-ROUND So will I. Goodbye, Mrs. Wilberforce. Thanks for
    everything.

He turns to pick up the case again

Marcus approaches

MARCUS Mrs. Wilberforce. What can I say? (*pause*) Ta-ta.

*He moves away, and once more his scarf is trapped beneath Mrs.
Wilberforce's foot*

MARCUS (CONT'D) Ha, ha. It's a shame this little tango of ours is
   soon to be a thing of the past.

*He yanks it just as One-Round is passing with the trunk. One-Round
trips over the suddenly taut scarf and the trunk falls and smashes open
on the floor*

*The money explodes out into the living room, falling like confetti around
the stunned men*

MAJOR AHHHHHH!!!!

Pause

MARCUS I suppose you're wondering... what's the story with all the
   money.

Harry and Louis enter behind him and are frozen to the spot

MARCUS (CONT'D) Hello, everyone! Nothing to worry about.

Louis slams the door

MARCUS (CONT'D) Major, could you explain about the money while
   we clean up? One-Round, could you escort Mrs. Wilberforce to the
   kitchen?

*One-Round picks her up like an object and carries her into the kitchen.
The still shaken Major follows behind*

MAJOR Explain about the...explain...but, but, but...

The rest of the gang desperately shovel money back into the trunk.

MAJOR (CONT'D) Mrs. Wilberforce, it's all very embarrassing. We
   have all been saving as a group to buy...special strings. Imported from
   Egypt. Quite expensive. They're made of ostriches.

Back in THE SITTING-ROOM:

LOUIS What are we going to do?
MARCUS We're going to go!

LOUIS She saw the money! She'll talk! My picture's on file and so's
Harry's! (*to One-Round*) And yours! If they take her down to the
gallery, she'll shop us! They've got our fingers and thumbs! What are
we going to do?

The Professor stops dead, and the other men stop too and stare at him

MARCUS I'll talk to her.
LOUIS You can talk to her all you want, it doesn't change—
MARCUS Louis. I'll talk to her.

*But Marcus is already walking into the kitchen, his demeanour changing
completely*

MARCUS (CONT'D) (*oleaginously charming*) Mrs. Wilberforce! How
embarrassing that you had to see that ridiculous display!
MAJOR I was just telling her about the ostriches.

He gestures "play along". Marcus stares at him

MAJOR (CONT'D) You know. The special strings?
MARCUS Stand down, Major.

The Major goes to the sitting-room

MRS. WILBERFORCE I still don't quite understand...
MARCUS It's all very simple, Mrs. Wilberforce.
MRS. WILBERFORCE I am...confused.
MARCUS Completely understandable.
MRS. WILBERFORCE ...all that money...
MARCUS I know!
MRS. WILBERFORCE What are you doing with so much money?
MARCUS Well, it's a long and complicated story Mrs. Wilberforce... I
can't imagine you'll be able to follow it, but nevertheless...

He pauses for effect

MARCUS (CONT'D) ...you see, being in a quintet is actually a lot
more expensive than you'd think...Recently, we put an advertisement
out in the *Ham and High* looking for a backer who would provide us
with the means by which...

One-Round comes in

ONE-ROUND We've got all the money from the robbery back in the case.

Beat. Marcus stares at her

MARCUS I don't suppose there's any chance you didn't hear that.
MRS.WILBERFORCE The robbery! (*the truth dawns*) Professor Marcus!
MARCUS Thought not.
MRS.WILBERFORCE I am shocked by this revelation! Shocked and appalled! Why, you're musicians!

Marcus says nothing

MRS.WILBERFORCE (CONT'D) You...you are musicians, aren't you?

Marcus bows his head in shame

MRS.WILBERFORCE (CONT'D) (*reeling*) You're...you're not...but I thought...I thought...

The doorbell rings

MAJOR Nyahhahhh!!
LOUIS (*shouts from sitting-room*) Who's that?
MAJOR People! Old ladies! It's a swarm of old ladies!
MRS. WILBERFORCE My friends. They're here for the concert.

One-Round is standing by the door

ONE-ROUND What do I do?
MARCUS It's three o'clock! That's not teatime!
MRS. WILBERFORCE It's our teatime.
MARCUS Teatime is five!
MRS. WILBERFORCE Our teatime is three. We're old. We get up at four thirty!
MARCUS That's a ridiculous time for teatime! You can't just have teatime whenever! Teatime is five! Harry, when's teatime?
HARRY Four, isn't it?

Another knock on the door

ONE-ROUND What do I do?

MARCUS Teatime is five!

MAJOR You're both wrong. Teatime is six! High tea is six o'clock. (*rounds on Mrs. Wilberforce*) You're making a mockery of teatime!

ONE-ROUND What do I do?

MRS. WILBERFORCE Oh, this is terrible, just terrible! What will they say? It will be a scandal!

MARCUS Mrs. Wilberforce, there is no need for any of them to know.

MRS. WILBERFORCE But I must tell them. I must!

He holds her by the shoulders. He's desperate, but composed

MARCUS Would you promise me to... to at least wait until your companions leave before we address the terrible problem of the money? I believe there's a clear moral course we can take. It's just a matter of thrashing one out.

MRS. WILBERFORCE But they are expecting a concert!

MARCUS ...and they shall have one.

Everyone freezes and stares at Marcus

MARCUS (CONT'D) Everyone, get your instruments!

LOUIS What? Are you insane?

MARCUS Just do as I say, Louis. Unless you want to use your popgun on a room full of old ladies. The Blue Rinse Massacre, they'll call it.

All the men retrieve their instruments

MARCUS (CONT'D) The door, One-Round!

MRS. WILBERFORCE (*entering from kitchen*) What are you going to do?

MARCUS Hard to explain. You're going to have to trust me.

MRS. WILBERFORCE How can I trust you?

MARCUS Mrs. Wilberforce, have I been anything other than a gentleman while staying here?

MRS. WILBERFORCE Well, yes, you executed a violent robbery.

MARCUS Aside from that, Mrs. Wilberforce!

MRS. WILBERFORCE I suppose...

MARCUS Good! One-Round?

One-Round nods and opens the door

A gaggle of old ladies suddenly swarm in and start to surround the

*'musicians', talking excitedly about the impending musical programme.
Louis is particuarly freaked out*

LOUIS Gahhhh!
MARCUS Ladies! Ladies, PLEASE do not speak to the musicians!
They require utmost concentration to perform! Please take your seats
immediately!

The women all look shocked and excited

MRS. TROMLEYTON Oh! Oh, yes, of course! Hello! I'm Mrs.
Tromleyton...
MARCUS Madam, I must insist you find your seat!
MRS.TROMLEYTON Oh! Yes!

They all sit

LOUIS Marcus, what are we going to do?!
MRS. WILBERFORCE Please don't embarrass me any more than you
already have!
MARCUS Embarrass you? Mrs. Wilberforce, I'm about to give your
friends the teatime of their lives.

Everyone finally settles and there is silence

*Marcus walks up to a mirror and stares at himself. He swallows hard.
Then he adjusts his cuffs like a conductor, and turns.*

*The ladies applaud immediately. He raises a hand and they stop
clapping*

MARCUS (CONT'D) Ladies and Gentlemen. Or at least... ladies. Allow
me first of all to pay tribute to the musicians who will be dazzling you
this fine teatime.

He walks up to One-Round

MARCUS (CONT'D) Mister Desmond Lawson.
ONE-ROUND I'm Mister Lawson.
MARCUS Yes, you are. Don't let his enormous dimensions fool you.
Mister Lawson may have the powerful body of a farm worker, but he
has the gentle, precise hands of a watchmaker.

The old ladies are incredibly excited by this. One-Round stares at his hands

He moves on to Major Courtney

MARCUS (CONT'D) I give you Major Courtney. He served his country with honour during the war, but tonight his only desire is to serve you.

Mrs. Tromleyton starts hyperventilating

The women applaud as Major Courtney bows. He moves on to Harry

MARCUS (CONT'D) Harold Robinson. Ladies, with his instrument, he can reach into your blouse and steal your soul.

Harry winks at them

The old ladies applaud

MARCUS (CONT'D) Louis! The Rumanian genius! Wild! Tempestuous! A dangerous figure! With his violin, he is a devil sent from hell to seduce you!

Louis bows and clicks his heels

The women are VERY interested in this and clap even louder. Mrs. Tromleyton nearly faints

MARCUS (CONT'D) I...am Professor Marcus, the conductor...and also the composer of the music you are about to hear. Now. I must warn you before we begin. I am a controversial figure in modern music.

The ladies are enthralled. The men totally flummoxed

MARCUS (CONT'D) Some have even gone so far as to call me... insane. True, the composition you are about to hear is a difficult piece. Quite often, it doesn't even look like the musicians know how to play their instruments! "Everything sounds out of tune and random!", was the opinion of a critic in one of the lesser broadsheets; "a hateful cacophony", was another. Yes, the barbarians of Fleet Street have had their fun with me all right! But tonight, ladies... tonight you will be my judge!

The ladies rumble in an excited way

MARCUS (CONT'D) So now, I beg of you. Listen, with the most
refined part of your ear, and ask yourself the question? Am I truly
insane? Or am I... a genius? Ladies! I present to you a little number I
call... 'Teatime is Five'!

*He turns and raises his baton. And the band start madly scratching at
their instruments as...*

...THE CURTAIN FALLS

ACT II

THE CURTAIN RISES...

...and the concert is coming to an end. An awful miserable cacophonous racket

Everyone stops except One-Round, who plays the opening notes of the minuet again

Once again, he gets to the fourth note and it ends the concert on a tuneless drone

The ladies are sitting there, in a slightly horrified trance

Then, they break into spontaneous, rapturous applause.

Mrs. Wilberforce sits on her hands

MARCUS Thank you! Thank you!

MRS. TROMLEYTON Professor. That was...words cannot... I have never heard anything like it. Extraordinary!

MARCUS Thank you, madam. What did you think of the Stiranko passage in the third movement? I worry it is somewhat tart.

MRS. TROMLEYTON No, no! Well, perhaps, but overall, the grandeur of the piece, the ambition, the sheer abundance of ideas more than makes up for it!

MARCUS (*bowing*) You are as wise as a man, Madam.

MRS. TROMLEYTON Oh! Thank you!

Louis is surrounded by elderly fans

LOUIS I want to stop talking to these old ladies!

MARCUS We should perhaps retire. Ladies! Performance can be terribly draining. But we shall return in a few months for a proper discussion of some of the issues raised by the piece. Thank you!

MRS. TROMLEYTON Louisa, that was wonderful. Thank you.

MRS. WILBERFORCE (*slightly stunned*) Oh...thank you, Jane. Thank you all!

The men usher the women out. The women trying to shake their hands the whole time. They have all left, except Mrs. Tromleyton, who turns in the doorway

MRS. TROMLEYTON Once again! Words cannot express...

Marcus slams the door on her. Mrs. Wilberforce is still sitting stunned. Marcus goes over to One-Round, and the others

MARCUS (*sotto*) Get the cases upstairs. (*to Mrs. Wilberforce*) Aaaah, Mrs. Wilberforce. A triumph, I think you'll agree.
MRS. WILBERFORCE I do not agree. I most certainly do not.
MARCUS What? Your friends loved it! It'll be a talking point for years!
MRS. WILBERFORCE I...I don't understand how they could have. It was horrible, just horrible!

One-Round picks up the cases, and trudges up to the Professor's rooms

MARCUS Being fooled by art is one of the primary pleasures afforded the middle class. They love it. They can't get enough of it.
MRS. WILBERFORCE It was dreadful. Indeed, if music is a reflection of one's inner soul, as I believe it to be, then all of you...

...she looks them all over

MRS. WILBERFORCE (CONT'D)...should be ashamed of yourselves.

The men stare at their feet

LOUIS (*to Marcus*) You know what we're going to have to do...
MRS.WILBERFORCE Yes, I'm calling the police.
MARCUS (*to Louis*) There must be another way.
MRS. WILBERFORCE (*crosses to phone*) No, I am calling the police.
MARCUS (*intercepts her*) Mrs. Wilberforce, please... before casting us in to the fiery abyss... has it occurred to you to wonder why five men such as ourselves should be driven to crime? Why we would risk apprehension, public humiliation, disgrace?
MRS. WILBERFORCE Well, that's not for me to—
MARCUS There is not one amongst us who is not burdened with responsibilities to others. Harry! Tell her your story!
HARRY Well, for a while I was with a woman who worked as a sort of 'paid companion'...

MARCUS NOT THAT STORY!

HARRY Oh! Oh, yeah! It's me... Mum? Oh, yeah! Me Mum, right, she's awful sick she is. I just wanted her to know that her little boy could take care of her. It's why I took the money, Miss.

MRS. WILBERFORCE What is the matter with her?

Marcus signals something. Harry picks up on it wrongly

HARRY She's blind.

Marcus signals again

HARRY (CONT'D)   She's insane. Sick! She's a blind insane sick woman...

Marcus puts his head in his hands

HARRY (CONT'D)   ...who enjoys washing her face...

MRS. WILBERFORCE I see...

HARRY (*really trying now*) And do you know what? Every night she calls me and tells me how much she's looking forward to seeing my face ...feeling my face... as I walk through the front door with a towel to dry ...her face...and some tablets or something for her wandering mind...and a little...a little puppy who I'm going to train up...to ...to be her eyes.

Pause

MARCUS Barely credible I know, but each of them could tell you a similar story. The Major, for instance. A war hero. He bravely escaped from occupied France in nothing but his wife's borrowed clothes.

MAJOR She sent them in a Red Cross parcel with a passport and some crisps. It was a black long sleeve dress with a peplum overskirt. Beautiful. Lined in satin. Satin cuffs too. The side zip had a—

MARCUS *THANK YOU*, Major. (*to Mrs. Wilberforce*) An extraordinary story of bravery and what has he to show for it? A measly Officer's pension. Is that a Country fit for Heroes?

MAJOR Though it shames me to admit it, I once ate from a bin.

Marcus glares at him: why the disgusting detail?

One-Round has appeared at the top of the stairs

MARCUS And Mr. Lawson!? He perhaps has the most heartrending story of all, don't you Mr. Lawson?

ONE-ROUND What? Oh, yeah, I... I... I don't think I should join in on this one. I'll only get it wrong.

MRS. WILBERFORCE What about you, Mr. Harvey?

LOUIS (*disgusted with this*) I run a Rumanian orphanage, how's that?

MARCUS I planned the robbery, Mrs. Wilberforce. I wanted to help them. I did it because I thought it was the right thing to do, and I still believe that. Surely you see that there is such a thing as... as a good crime?

Pause as Mrs. Wilberforce thinks this over

MR. WILBERFORCE No. No, I do not.

MARCUS Mrs. Wilberforce, the Major's eating dog food from bins!!

MAJOR Well, I never said dog food.

MARCUS Harry's blind mother is madly washing her face as we speak!

LOUIS (*disinterested*) "Won't somebody think of the children."

MARCUS How could you condemn these men to such disgrace?

MRS. WILBERFORCE Poverty is no disgrace.

MARCUS But it's a bit of a nuisance. Besides, they won't even miss the money! It's all insured, and what we have here will only amount to a farthing on everyone's premiums. What harm is a farthing? We're just being more creative with the money. What would the public do with it? They'd only waste it.

MRS. WILBERFORCE But it is wrong.

MARCUS Let me put it this way. How is, say, robbing a bank any different to founding one?

MRS. WILBERFORCE One is a crime and one is not.

MARCUS Which one?

MRS. WILBERFORCE I'm sorry, you're just trying to confuse me.

She moves towards the telephone

MARCUS Mrs. Wilberforce, may I remind you of your own culpability in this matter?

MRS. WILBERFORCE But I didn't steal the money.

MARCUS Oh, but you did. You transported the money back from the station.

This pulls her up short

MRS. WILBERFORCE Wh—What?

MARCUS Yes. Without you, the plan would have fallen apart. You were an essential component.

HARRY That's right! She carried the lolly!

MARCUS (*to the others*) She was ignorant of the plan, of course.

MAJOR Ignorance in the sight of the law is no excuse. Believe me, I'm always pleading ignorance.

MARCUS Oh, dear! I think the Major's right! You see, Mrs. Wilberforce? ...We're all in this together.

HARRY Do you know what they do to old ladies in prison? They eat them!

Marcus gives Harry a whack to shut him up

MARCUS It's certainly no picnic in prison for a woman of your advanced years.

The parrot SQUAWKS!

MARCUS (CONT'D) And you have dependents too. Am I the only one thinking of General Gordon?

MRS. WILBERFORCE Oh!

MARCUS But don't worry!

HARRY We won't let them get you, Mrs. Wilberforce!

MAJOR You're one of us now!

MRS. WILBERFORCE But what can we do? Where will we go? Oh, dear, oh dear!

LOUIS You're not doing her any favours, you know.

Marcus approaches her, gently

MARCUS You see, Mrs. Wilberforce. The police are the last people we want to bring in on this. You see that. You see that, don't you? Couldn't you—just this once—look the other way? We would make it worth your while of course.

HARRY Yeah! We'll all chip in! Right, lads?

The Major and One-Round agree but Louis looks alarmed

MARCUS Think what you could do with your share of the money! That trip to America! The treatment for General Gordon! Within your means at last! America! What an adventure for a woman of your mature years. To live, Mrs. Wilberforce! You could live at last!

The men await her answer

Mrs. Wilberforce takes some time to compose herself

Finally...

MRS. WILBERFORCE No.

Marcus's shoulders slump. This was his last card

MARCUS Ah.
MRS. WILBERFORCE That is my final word.
MARCUS Yes.
MRS. WILBERFORCE I'm sorry. I realise what it means for all of you.
  But there are things in life we must do, no matter how unpleasant.

Pause

MARCUS I must say, I'm coming round to that way of thinking.
MRS. WILBERFORCE Then we are agreed? The best course is to turn
  the whole matter over to the authorities?
MARCUS Agreed. In fact... I will phone the police myself. I ask only
  to be allowed to do it in private, so that there is no witness to my
  shame.
MRS. WILBERFORCE Of course. I am sorry, Professor, but were I
  to ignore this, I should never be able to look my husband in the eye
  again. Where is the money?
ONE-ROUND It's upstairs.
MRS. WILBERFORCE To keep you and your men from temptation,
  Professor, I shall sit with it, while you ring the police.
MARCUS One-Round, could you accompany Mrs. Wilberforce and
  give her any assistance she requires?
MRS. WILBERFORCE Who is this One-Round?
ONE-ROUND It's... it's me. Mister Lawson.

*Mrs. Wilberforce stares at him for a second, then turns, walks up the
stairs, and enters the Professor's rooms. One-Round follows and closes
the door behind him*

*The men stand there, looking at Marcus. The atmosphere is suddenly
very grave*

Pause

LOUIS You know what we have to do.

He turns to the others

LOUIS (CONT'D) You all do. All these fun and games... we're just
   losing time.

The men all look at each other

LOUIS (CONT'D) You *know* what we have to *do*.

UPSTAIRS...

*While One-Round watches, Mrs. Wilberforce checks that the money is
in the cello case*

As she moves across the room, she knocks against the gramophone

*There is a horrible SCRATCHING noise, and then the familiar piece
begins*

She looks at One-Round, who is deeply ashamed

She opens the door

MRS. WILBERFORCE You may leave, Mr La—You may leave.

*One-Round takes out a wad of money from his coat, and puts it on the
chair, then exits the room*

DOWNSTAIRS...

MARCUS It ought to look like an accident.

One-Round is on the landing

ONE-ROUND What ought to look like an accident?
HARRY Suicide, maybe. We could leave a note: "I couldn't take it
   anymore!".
MAJOR Makes sense. She's obviously very lonely. It might be a
   blessing.
ONE-ROUND What might be a blessing?
MARCUS Don't dress it up, Major. This is a terrible thing that must be
   done. But it must be done. She just won't play the game.

ONE-ROUND (*increasingly disturbed, coming down the stairs*) What game? What's goin' on?

LOUIS Who's going to do it?

MARCUS Well, there is one obvious candidate...

LOUIS Me? No, no, no.

MARCUS You said yourself you hate old ladies.

LOUIS I didn't get into this business to kill old ladies. You brought her in, you take her out!

MARCUS What good are you, then? To us! What's your role if not that!?

LOUIS If it was one of you lot, I'd kill you like that! (*he snaps his fingers*) But her? I find it distasteful. It's beneath me!

MARCUS Well, someone's go to do it! We can't just sit here drinking tea and wait for her to die of natural causes!

ONE-ROUND (*implacably*) I don't like this.

MARCUS Oh, One-Round, neither do we! I know it seems like a terrible thing we're considering, but put yourself in her shoes. She's old. Imagine being old! Old people, they don't know what's going on half the time. They forget how to amuse themselves! If you don't talk to them, they just sit there! And because they don't contribute anything, people resent them! Is that what you want? Do you want her to be resented?

ONE-ROUND (*totally befuddled*) Eh... oh... I...

MARCUS You are condemning her to a dreadful fate, One-Round. Old, alone and resented! Haunting these rooms like a wraith in a pinny! And it would all be on your shoulders. You're a strong man but can you carry that?

ONE-ROUND Oh... well...

MARCUS Have a think about it, One-Round! It's quite complicated.

One-Round goes to think about it

MARCUS (CONT'D) It has to be one of us.

HARRY Eeny meeny miney...

LOUIS We're not doing eeny meeny for this!

HARRY Why not?

LOUIS I've never liked eeny meeny. It's imperfect! You could start in such a way that you know you're not going to choose yourself!

HARRY Scissor, paper, stone!?

MARCUS There's five of us! How would that work?

HARRY We could have a tournament!

MARCUS We don't have time for a scissors paper stone tournament!

Throughout all this, the Major has been quiet, so when he speaks, everyone else stops talking

MAJOR Gentlemen. There is no need for any of this.

He steps forward

MAJOR (CONT'D) I shall do the deed.
MARCUS Claude, are you sure?
MAJOR There comes a point in every man's life when he has to stop running away. If I don't have the steel to kill a little old lady, why, then, I am no man, sir!
LOUIS I like you, Courtney! I don't understand why you were fondling that dress and talking about being a lady, but I like you!
MAJOR I'll make it as painless as possible.

He leaves the room. He goes upstairs

LOUIS What'll we do with the body?
MARCUS Newcastle goods train. It's fairly dependable. Chuck her onto that.
LOUIS Good for me.

UPSTAIRS...

Mrs. Wilberforce is watching the cello case carefully when Major Courtney comes in. He locks the door and stands behind her threateningly. He gently coughs

MRS. WILBERFORCE Professor?
MAJOR No, it's me, Mrs. Wilberforce. The men are all playing cards and I took the chance to slip away.
MRS. WILBERFORCE It's no use asking for the money, Major.
MAJOR No, no, no, you mustn't give me the money. You see, Mrs. Wilberforce, I am a police officer...
MRS. WILBERFORCE What?
MAJOR *Shhh!* Yes, I've been sent to infiltrate the gang. I'm a member of Scotland Yard's "Ghost Squad".
MRS. WILBERFORCE I've never heard of them.
MAJOR Exactly.
MRS. WILBERFORCE Well, why don't you arrest them?
MAJOR On my own? Mrs. Wilberforce, these are dangerous men. And I am unarmed!

MRS. WILBERFORCE But you could escape! And you could bring
 reinforcements!
MAJOR Escape? How?
MRS. WILBERFORCE Out the window!
MAJOR Of course! And I'll leave all the money here with you!
MRS. WILBERFORCE No, you must take the money!
MAJOR What, *me* take the money?
MRS. WILBERFORCE Yes! It will be safer with you!

Pause

MAJOR You're right.

She hands him the cello case

*He clasps it to his breast and then bows his head to her knee, like a
knight before a queen*

MAJOR (CONT'D) Farewell, Mrs. Wilberforce! I shall return within
 the hour! (*looks out window*) God's teeth, that is quite a drop, isn't it?
 I don't remember it being quite so...eh....

DOWNSTAIRS...

LOUIS Can we trust him?
MARCUS Oh, I've known the Major for years, Louis. If there's anyone
 who... who...
LOUIS What?
MARCUS ...What the hell are we doing? No, we can't trust him! He's
 a f**king conman!

Luckily, General Gordon SQUAWKS over the offending word

He stands up and runs upstairs

*He bounds up the stairs, and tries the door. It's locked. He bangs on the
door*

UPSTAIRS...

*The Major can't get the case through the window, so he opens it and
starts stuffing bundles of money into his jacket*

Marcus bangs on the door again

MAJOR Cover for me!
MRS. WILBERFORCE Oh! Yes! Of course!

She walks over and takes a blanket from the bed and drapes it over the Major's shoulders

MAJOR What? No, Mrs. Wilberforce. Lie!
MRS. WILBERFORCE Lie?
MAJOR Yes, lie! Lie. At the door!
MRS. WILBERFORCE Major, I don't care how cold you are, I am not a draft excluder.
MAJOR *Tell lies!* Tell lies! I really can't be any clearer than that, Mrs. Wilberforce!
MRS. WILBERFORCE Oh, of course! (*at the door*) Hello?
MARCUS Mrs. Wilberforce?
MRS. WILBERFORCE Yes?
MARCUS Hello, um....
MRS. WILBERFORCE Hello!
MARCUS Yes, ah....
MRS. WILBERFORCE Yes?
MARCUS Hello, is the—
MRS. WILBERFORCE Hello, yes.
MARCUS Is the — is the Major within?

Pause

MRS. WILBERFORCE He is within. He...

She looks to the Major for help. The Major urges her to continue

MRS. WILBERFORCE (CONT'D) ... he's not a policeman!
MARCUS I beg your pardon!
MRS. WILBERFORCE He's not a policeman!
MARCUS He's not a policeman. That's good to know. May I have a word with him?
MRS. WILBERFORCE No, he's... he's having a sleep.
MARCUS A sleep! How sweet! (*to Louis*) Harry! Check outside! One-Round! Get this open!

Harry runs downstairs

MAJOR Ha, ha. Once again, Mrs. Wilberforce, your police force thanks you, your country thanks you, ehm... I'll have to leave the rest. But this is very useful evidence, very useful indeed!

He is half through the window

MAJOR (CONT'D) You do have some beautiful dresses, Mrs. Wilberforce. You know, in another life... we may even have been friends.

He leaves through the window, travelling upwards

One-Round runs up and—snap—the door is suddenly open. Marcus, One-Round and Louis rush in, and... The Major is nowhere to be seen

THE SET REVOLVES...

OUTSIDE ON THE ROOF...

...we see The Major clambering onto the roof from the window. It's dark now. Moonlight...

Marcus sticks his head out the window

MARCUS Oh, Major. We're not going to have to chase you like an escaped parrot, are we?

Louis pushes Marcus from the window, takes his jacket off and then climbs out himself

The Major tries to get away. Eventually, The Major is cornered between the chimneypot and Louis

MAJOR Now, now, Louis! Stay away.
LOUIS It's all right. Come on. Let's go down.
MAJOR I... I... I don't want to. I want to sit up here.
LOUIS You don't want to sit up there. That's silly.
MAJOR I do. I want to...I want to look at the world.
LOUIS You want to look at the world.

Beat. Louis sighs, shrugs, and takes out a cigarette. He offers it to the Major. The Major reaches out and takes it gingerly

They start to smoke

MAJOR Hello, Harry.
HARRY (*from below*) Hello!
LOUIS S'OK, Harry! I'm dealing with it.

Pause

MAJOR Always liked it round here.
LOUIS Oh, yes?
MAJOR Oh, yes. Always liked King's Cross. It has a reputation
    but I've found people here to be lovely. Very compassionate. Very
    understanding, if you get my meaning.
LOUIS I don't but carry on.
MAJOR In general, people can be cruel if they detect even a whiff of...
    originality. But not in some of the places round here. No, I've always
    loved King's Cross.

Pause

LOUIS Good place for a holiday?
MAJOR I'd say so.
LOUIS Well.

Louis puts his cigarette out

*The Major seems to decide something. He stands up and assumes a
ridiculous boxer's stance*

MAJOR Come on, then!

We hear the sound of an approaching TRAIN

LOUIS Oh, Major. Really? Why don't you just come downstairs?
MAJOR Ha! You'd like that wouldn't you? No, no, there comes a time.
    This is where I take my stand!

*Louis sighs and moves towards him. The Major immediately turns and
starts scrambling up the chimney*

LOUIS Oh, Major, there's nowhere to go!
MAJOR I'm not coming down, you can't make me! I'll stay up here all
    night if that's what it...aaaaaarrggh!!

He grabs onto one of the chimneys and it crumbles under his hands. He pitches forward and falls off the side of the roof

There is a sickening KLANG, and the shrieking WHISTLE of the train

Louis looks over the roof top

Then he takes off his hat, in respect

THE SET REVOLVES...

UPSTAIRS...

The rest of the men, and Mrs. Wilberforce are in the Professor's rooms

MARCUS So the Major was a policeman.
ONE-ROUND Was he?
MARCUS That is a shocker.
MRS. WILBERFORCE Yes, yes, he infiltrated you!
HARRY Ouch! Ha, ha!
MRS. WILBERFORCE And I am afraid he exposed you, Professor.

Marcus sees Louis looking through the window. Louis shakes his head and indicates with his hand that the Major fell

MARCUS Exposed and infiltrated. What a terrible day I'm having.
MRS. WILBERFORCE He said you didn't phone the police. But it doesn't matter, because he's fetching reinforcements.
MARCUS Is he? Curses! Well, I suppose it's for the best.
MRS. WILBERFORCE In which case I shall take this money downstairs and wait for them.
MARCUS And how about a lovely cup of tea?
MRS. WILBERFORCE Oh! Of course!

She struggles out with the cello case

ONE-ROUND Let me help you, m'm.

Louis comes in through the window

MARCUS Where is he?
LOUIS Newcastle. On his way, at least.
MARCUS The goods train? How very efficient of you.

LOUIS Nothing to do with me. He fell onto it!
MARCUS Of course he did.
LOUIS He did! Right onto the train! I didn't touch him!

Marcus doesn't seem convinced

DOWNSTAIRS...

GENERAL GORDON Who's a naughty boy!
MRS. WILBERFORCE   I'm so sorry, General Gordon. All this
   commotion. You must be quite exhausted.

*One-Round puts the cello case down next to her chair, and starts back
up the stairs*

Mrs. Wilberforce settles in her chair and starts to sing softly to the bird

One-Round stops on the stairs when he hears her

MRS. WILBERFORCE (CONT'D) (*sings*)
                  Darling, I am growing old.
                  Silver threads among the gold.
                  Shine upon my brow today.

*She crosses to her chair and sits down. As she sings, her head starts to
nod*

*One-Round slowly starts to walk upstairs again. He looks like he's
puzzling something out*

MRS. WILBERFORCE (CONT'D)
                  Life is fading fast away.
                  But my darling you will be, will be...
                  Ever young and fresh to me....

She falls asleep

UPSTAIRS...

Marcus is deep in conversation with Harry

MARCUS ...it's why it makes total sense for you to take care of her.
   Don't you see, Harry, don't you see?

HARRY I don't see how my height comes into it.
MARCUS You're the perfect height to kill her!

One-Round enters the room, deep in thought, and puts on a jacket. It's Louis's, a few sizes too small for him

LOUIS Look at him. The poor, simple idiot. That's my jacket.
MARCUS Louis! Talk to him!
LOUIS Hm? Yes, yes, what are you, 23? Good age for it. My first, I was younger — but it's a good age.
MARCUS ...and to sweeten the pot, we'll give you a little something extra from the Major's share.
LOUIS (*putting his jacket on*) How do you want to do it? Do you want my knife? How about a gun? Violin strings? That would be... ah, ironical!
HARRY One-Round, where is she?
ONE-ROUND Mrs. Lopsided? She's nodded off.

Harry looks around and sees the pillow from earlier

HARRY I'll bring her this. For her head.

He goes to leave the room

MARCUS Oh, and Harry?
HARRY Yes?
MARCUS Try anything and Louis will kill you like he killed the Major.
LOUIS I didn't kill the Major but yes, I will kill you.

The others sit in the room and he goes downstairs. On the stairs, he stops. He looks at the sleeping Mrs. Wilberforce. He loosens his tie, and takes it off

He starts to walk slowly towards her...

UPSTAIRS...

ONE-ROUND I've been thinking.
MARCUS I'm sorry?
ONE-ROUND I said... I've been thinking.
MARCUS That's great news! Well done, One-Round!
ONE-ROUND No-one hurts Mrs. Lopsided.

MARCUS Well, now One-Round, rushing to—

One-Round pokes his finger into Marcus's chest. Hard

ONE-ROUND No-one. Hurts. Mrs. Lopsided.

The three men look at each other

DOWNSTAIRS...

Harry is near Mrs. Wilberforce. He has the pillow in his hands. But then Mrs. Wilberforce shudders, and he stops...

MRS. WILBERFORCE (*stirring*) Arthur?
HARRY Er... yes?
MRS. WILBERFORCE I do hope I haven't let you down, Arthur.
HARRY No, no, you're doing very well, er... my love. Just... go back to sleep, eh?

He approaches her but then spots something

HARRY (CONT'D) Oh, would you look at that.

He starts furiously cleaning a spot behind her

UPSTAIRS...

One-Round is still towering over Marcus

ONE-ROUND This is the new plan. We take the money, we go.
MARCUS Yes, wonderful. But if Mrs. Wilberforce talks...
ONE-ROUND   WE TAKE OUR CHANCES if she talks. Where's Harry?

Beat

MARCUS Why 'One-Round', One-Round?
ONE-ROUND What?
MARCUS How did you earn the sobriquet?
ONE-ROUND The what?
MARCUS The nickname. Your nickname. What people call you. I've always wondered but I never thought to ask.
ONE-ROUND Why do you wanna know all of a sudden?

MARCUS Idle fancy.

ONE-ROUND Mm. Well, it is a bit of a funny story, actually.

MARCUS *(pulling up a chair)* Take your time. I'm honestly fascinated.

ONE-ROUND Well at first it was because I used to put people down in the first round.

His hands, almost involuntarily, start to move through the air as he assumes a boxer's stance

ONE-ROUND (CONT'D) Wouldn't even have to hit them too hard. Just pop. And that was them. Won a load of fights that way. So they called me One-Round. Then I met Mr. Falton, and he explained how I could make more money if it was me who went down in the first round. You know. On purpose. Just let the other fella work on me a little bit... and then go down. Lost a load of fights that way. So they... so they called me One-Round.

He frowns, looking confused

ONE-ROUND (CONT'D) The money was better, though, and I used to like the music.

MARCUS What music, One-Round?

ONE-ROUND The music they played between me being hit and me hitting the canvas. At least, I think they played music. I certainly heard music.

DOWNSTAIRS...

Mrs. Wilberforce stirs again. Harry tenses

HARRY Gah!

He walks away and slaps his face, and comes back to himself somewhat

He looks over at Mrs. Wilberforce

HARRY (CONT'D) Why couldn't you take a bit of the money? It's all a racket, innit? I never met a single soul who wasn't on the take. Coppers, housewives, the posh. You call it a crime, what we done, but... we're just doing our bit.

He sighs and walks up behind her, raising the pillow

He's right behind her now but then sees something and stops. A mark on the chair? He licks his finger and starts to rub it

HARRY (CONT'D) Tsk.

He licks the end and rubs harder. A stubborn little stain

UPSTAIRS...

ONE-ROUND (*looks around suddenly*) Where's Harry?
MARCUS (*quickly*) If a tree falls in the forest, does it make a sound?
ONE-ROUND What?
MARCUS If a tree falls in the forest, does it make a sound?
ONE-ROUND (*getting up*) Yeah. A crashing sound.
MARCUS (*really fast...*) But there's no-one around to hear it. How does it make a sound if no one's around to hear it?
ONE-ROUND The birds hear it! STOP TALKING! WHERE'S HARRY?

One-Round opens the door and charges downstairs

DOWNSTAIRS...

Harry is still rubbing the stain furiously

HARRY There! Bloody hell.

One-Round enters to see...

Harry stepping back from Mrs. Wilberforce's chair, holding the pillow

Mrs. Wilberforce's hand falling to the side

HARRY (CONT'D) She's done in.

One-Round stares at him. His fists clench

HARRY (CONT'D) Cor. I'm still shaking. Come on, let's—
ONE-ROUND You did it.
HARRY What?
ONE-ROUND You killed Mrs. Lopsided!
HARRY What? No, no, no... she's...
ONE-ROUND No-one hurts Mrs. Lopsided!

HARRY No, no, I never! It's not in me, One-Round! It's not in me!

One-Round grabs him and throws him into the bannisters, which he goes through head first

He staggers backwards, blood running down his face

One-Round goes for him. Harry starts to run. He manages to make it back up the stairs and into the room with Louis and Marcus. He locks the door. One-Round slowly comes after him

DOWNSTAIRS...

Mrs. Wilberforce has woken with the sounds of the struggle. She stands up, unsteadily, and starts to make her way upstairs

UPSTAIRS...

Marcus stares at the bloody figure of Harry

MARCUS How's it going?
HARRY Tell him! Tell him I didn't do it! He's gone mad!

One-Round SMASHES the door in

He picks up Harry up and throws him against the blackboard

One-Round takes the board off and starts to hit Harry with it, chasing him towards the bed. It smashes over Harry's head

HARRY (CONT'D) One-Round! No! I didn't do anything! She's asleep!
ONE-ROUND What do you think I am, STUPID OR SOMETHING?

One-Round beats Harry to death with the blackboard

Mrs. Wilberforce comes in

ONE-ROUND (CONT'D) Mrs. Lopsided?
MRS. WILBERFORCE Mister Lawson! Whatever are you doing? What was that sound? And who on earth is Mrs. Lopsided? I hope you gentlemen are not having second thoughts on turning yourselves in to the police.

MARCUS No, no, we're being very good.
MRS. WILBERFORCE Where is Mister Robinson?
ONE-ROUND He's... he's done in.

The TRAIN PASSES, clattering noisily and re-producing the BEDLAM of before. The lights FLICKER

When the lights come back on. One-Round has just come back from the window. One of Harry's shoes is on the floor. He chucks that out the window too

ONE-ROUND (CONT'D) Sorry, Harry.

Marcus and Louis are on the landing

Mrs. Wilberforce is BANGING THE PIPES IN THE KITCHEN...

ON THE LANDING...

They eye the cello case in the sitting-room

LOUIS I mean, we are going to kill her, right? We have to!
MARCUS ...and One-Round?
LOUIS Don't worry about One-Round, I'll do him. But you'll have to do the old lady. I can't do the old lady.

Marcus thinks it over

MARCUS All right! A two way split! But we stop after that! The atmosphere's getting terribly morbid.
LOUIS Agreed.
MARCUS Let's all get out to the car. Once he's in, stab him in the neck.
LOUIS I think I will decide where to stab him, thank you very much!
MARCUS (*losing it*) It's just a suggestion, Louis! Not everything's a criticism! I'm sure wherever you choose to stab him will be perfectly fine!

One-Round comes out of the Professor's rooms

MARCUS (CONT'D) (*changing immediately*) Ah, One-Round. Shall we away to the car?
ONE-ROUND Yeah. We will away.

They all three walk jauntily down the stairs

MARCUS We were just saying, a three-way split. So that's something.

DOWNSTAIRS...

ONE-ROUND Yeah.

They get to the sitting-room

ONE-ROUND (CONT'D) Why aren't you saying anything, Louis?
LOUIS I have nothing to say.
ONE-ROUND You always have something to say.
LOUIS This time I don't.
ONE-ROUND Not going to call me a big ape or something?
LOUIS Why would I do that?
ONE-ROUND It's what you usually do. What's different about now?
LOUIS I don't know what you're talking about!
ONE-ROUND How were you going to do it? In the car, yeah? Were you
    going to stab me or shoot me?

More BANGING FROM THE KITCHEN...

MARCUS Change of plan, Louis! Deal with him! Now, now, now!

Marcus runs over to Louis, who reaches instinctively for his pistol

He fumbles around desperately in his pocket. It's not there!

One-Round holds up Louis' revolver

LOUIS How did you—
ONE-ROUND Not as stupid as I look, am I? Big dumb lunk trying on
    the wrong jacket.

Marcus literally dances over to One-Round and faces Louis

MARCUS Well done, One-Round! You saw through his charade!
ONE-ROUND Back over there, Professor.

Marcus slowly walks back to stand beside an outraged Louis

He looks at Louis and shrugs an apology

ONE-ROUND (CONT'D) So, Professor? Not so stupid after all, am I?
MARCUS One question, One-Round. Why are you holding the gun in
  such a strange way?

One-Round looks somewhat nervous at this

MARCUS (CONT'D) Is your finger perhaps too big to fit through the
  trigger guard?

One-Round suddenly looks worried

LOUIS Ahhhhh! That's it, isn't it? Hold still.
ONE-ROUND What?

Louis throws something at One-Round

THUNK. A KNIFE is sticking out the centre of One-Round's head

One-Round stands there for a second

ONE-ROUND (CONT'D) Has something happened?!

He walks over to the mirror and looks in it

ONE-ROUND (CONT'D) Awwwww!!! What'd you that for?
MARCUS Brilliant. You missed his brain.
ONE-ROUND Louis!
LOUIS You were going to shoot me. I'm...er... I'm sorry.
ONE-ROUND It's all right. What were we talking about?
MARCUS Oh, nothing very interesting. Well...this is awkward now.
ONE-ROUND Oh, I know! I was telling you how much I enjoyed this
  job.
MARCUS Oh?
ONE-ROUND Yeah, I did, I really did! Next job, can we have music
  again?
MARCUS Of course, One-Round.

One-Round, dully, picks up the cello

ONE-ROUND Cuz I really think I'm getting the hang of this.

We hear a TRAIN approaching. The noise grows throughout...

As the blood continues to run down ONE-ROUND'S face, he attempts to play the first few notes of the minuet

Da, da, da, da...DA, da, da, da, da, da

Stiff, artless, but nonetheless, for the first and last time, One-Round manages to hit the note that his been evading him all week

He smiles and dies

Louis and Marcus stand there

LOUIS If only he had had a knife in his head sooner.
MARCUS Yes. Who knows what he might have achieved?

A TRAIN SCREAMS PAST... A terrifying sound. Lights flicker ON and OFF, DAZZLING the audience momentarily

When they come back on One-Round is gone. Everyone is gone

The house is EMPTY. The cello case is still in its place in the sitting room

The house creaks...

A knock on the Professor's door...

UPSTAIRS...

Mrs. Wilberforce opens the door, humming

MRS. WILBERFORCE (*calling out*) Tea's ready!

Marcus and Louis are together

MARCUS One-Round always said he wanted to visit the North.

They go in to his rooms

MARCUS (CONT'D) You know, Louis, I have a bone to pick with
  you.
LOUIS A what to what?
MARCUS Some of your criticisms. Of my plan. I've found them quite
  hurtful.

LOUIS Oh, really? You have? Oh, boo-hoo. Boo-hoo-hoo.

MARCUS The old lady was the masterstroke. We'd never have got it out of the station ourselves!

LOUIS Masterstroke!

MARCUS Yes, there were elements that noone could have forseen... But a two way split, Louis! I think we can both be pleased at least with that!

LOUIS It was a weak premise. You can't build anything on a weak premise.

MARCUS We have enough money to go comfortably on the run, and we have eliminated the colleagues that would be of the greatest danger to us were they to be taken into custody. To me, Sir, that is a successful plan and I deserve, I believe, some credit!

LOUIS What, you want me to give you a rave review? Here's your review. (*very deliberately*) As soon as you involved the old lady, the plan turned into the biggest piece of shit the world has ever seen. This reviewer will not be attending any more performances by the 'great' Professor Marcus.

Marcus stares at him

LOUIS (CONT'D) Anyway, come on, your turn to kill someone.

Louis sits down and starts messing around with his knife

MARCUS Oh, yes, of course.

He crosses to the bathroom and starts composing himself

LOUIS (*mumbling to himself*) Not even about the money any more. He's just fishing for praise!

MARCUS It does seem though, doesn't it, that everyone who attempts to dispatch the old dear to Newcastle ends up... (*giggles*) ...dispatched themselves.

Marcus pauses at the bathroom light

MARCUS (CONT'D) Perhaps it's time to break the sequence.

He quite deliberately switches the light off

THE HOUSE IS PLUNGED IN TO DARKNESS

A DAMP, rank smell is suddenly everywhere

UPSTAIRS...

Louis hits the deck, and starts to whimper. He crawls slowly in to a corner

Marcus walks slowly back to his rooms, whistling the Boccherini

MARCUS So tell me more about these stories.
LOUIS Turn the light on! Why is the light off?
MARCUS The old woman, the stories she told you. When you were a little boy. When you were hiding from the Germans. Tell me one!
LOUIS Marcus, turn on the light! Please!
MARCUS Cinderella's sister cutting her toes off so the shoe will fit? Her ruse discovered when blood starts dripping from the enchanted slipper? That's a good one.
LOUIS Marcus!
MARCUS Or The Juniper Tree! The little boy, killed by his stepmother, eaten in a stew by his father?

Marcus giggles

Sudden sparks light up Louis' face. Louis is trying to light a match

LOUIS Gah! Damn it!

We hear him fumbling for another match

LOUIS (CONT'D) Marcus! MARCUS! Say something!
MARCUS You shouldn't have criticised the plan, Louis.
LOUIS Marcus, if I had any criticisms, it were meant constructively. I hope you know that.

After a few moments, he lights a match, revealing a grinning Marcus standing behind him

Marcus brings something down around Louis' neck

Louis flails and drops the match

We hear a TRAIN start to approach

The dying light of the match barely illuminates the following

MARCUS (*in the darkness, over gurgling*) Oh, I do, Louis, I really
do. And I agree that a weak premise spells doom for most artistic
endeavours. But I still don't think you see the overall genius at work
here. Thank you for this opportunity, by the way. It's so refreshing to
be able to have a frank conversation with a critic. No, I agree that the
premise certainly wasn't flawless, but the ending Louis. Don't you
think the ending makes up for it? I get all the money, Louis. All the
money.

Louis is now quiet

We hear his body slam to the floor

The train passes. The smoke clears. Marcus is standing there

Mrs. Wilberforce knocks on the door

MRS. WILBERFORCE Hello? Professor?
MARCUS Ah, the angel of death!

He opens the door and steps outside with her

MRS. WILBERFORCE Where are your friends, Professor Marcus?
MARCUS Too ashamed to show their faces.
MRS. WILBERFORCE That is understandable. Come down and sit in
the warm, Professor. I have tea.
MARCUS Who can say no to tea?

He walks slowly down behind her

They then sit across from each other and drink

MARCUS (CONT'D) You're really a very nice person, aren't you, Mrs.
Wilberforce?
MRS. WILBERFORCE Well. It's not for me to say. We all do our best,
though, don't we?
MARCUS Not all of us.
MRS. WILBERFORCE There's a little bit of good in everyone. That's
what I've always thought.
MARCUS Yes.

He sips his tea

MARCUS (CONT'D) It seems to be what did for us, all right.

MRS. WILBERFORCE I'm sorry?

MARCUS Mrs. Wilberforce. I've come to a decision.

MRS. WILBERFORCE Oh, yes?

MARCUS Yes. I'm going to leave. And I'm going to take the money with me.

MRS. WILBERFORCE But Professor Marcus! You gave me your word!

MARCUS Sadly, my word is worth nothing.

MRS. WILBERFORCE But the police...

MARCUS The police aren't coming. The Major's word was worth even less than mine, I'm afraid. You're all alone, and I am a dangerous man. In fact...

Mrs. Wilberforce moves to stand from her chair, giving him a fright

MARCUS (CONT'D)   Don't!... Don't come any closer, Mrs. Wilberforce.

But she stands up and walks to the front door

MRS. WILBERFORCE You shall not pass, Professor!

She walks to the front door and blocks it. Marcus stares at her for a second

MARCUS I can go out the window. Ha! Didn't think of that, did you?

He starts up the stairs with the cello case. Mrs. Wilberforce follows behind, perhaps stepping on his scarf. He stumbles a bit, in fear

Now the situation seems to be that Mrs. Wilberforce is pursuing Marcus up the stairs

MARCUS (CONT'D)   Stay back! There's no need to get quite so close.

MRS. WILBERFORCE You shall not escape me, Professor!

Marcus whimpers. He runs into the room, gets out of the window, then reaches back in to grab the case

MARCUS You see, what you didn't realise...is that you're dealing with a very, very clever man.

He pulls the cello case after him and THUNK, it hits the frame

He turns it slightly. THUNK. It still won't go out the window

THUNK, THUNK, THUNK

Nothing works

MARCUS (CONT'D) Come on, come on, arrrgh!

It suddenly falls onto the floor as we hear him screaming outside

The set revolves and we see a...

TRAIN TUNNEL...

Marcus limps along through a train tunnel. It looks like he's broken his arm in the fall. His scarf hangs down behind him

MARCUS Diddle-iddle-um, dum-da-da-da—dadum. It was a good plan, shut up, Louis! It was a good plan, it was a very good plan.

We hear the approaching whistle of a train. Marcus starts to move

There is a horribly clear and final clicking sound as the tracks switch

Marcus is jerked back by his scarf, which has been caught in the tracks. He pulls at it, uselessly, giggling...

...finally, he gives up, exhausted, resigned

He lets go of the scarf

MARCUS (CONT'D) Oh, maybe it was a weak premise.

A train SCREAMS out of the tunnel...

THE SET REVOLVES...

DOWNSTAIRS...

Constable MacDonald is sitting, a notebook and a pen in his hand

Mrs. Wilberforce sits across from him

Constable MacDonald is taking notes

He stares at her

CONSTABLE MACDONALD The ghost squad.
MRS. WILBERFORCE Yes!
CONSTABLE MACDONALD I haven't heard of them.
MRS. WILBERFORCE Exactly.

Pause

CONSTABLE MACDONALD So let me just... these are the gentlemen
    I met? The musicians? The ones who gave that concert Mrs.
    Tromleyton's been raving about?
MRS. WILBERFORCE Yes.
CONSTABLE MACDONALD They're master criminals.
MRS. WILBERFORCE Yes. Although, they really were all very nice.
    The Professor... well, one might even describe him as a gentleman....
    now where did I put the...

She stands up and starts looking around

CONSTABLE MACDONALD And they all just...vanished, is that
    right?
MRS. WILBERFORCE Yes. That's right. Vanished.
CONSTABLE MACDONALD Mrs. Wilberforce, what are you looking
    for?
MRS. WILBERFORCE The money! I put it somewhere safe but I can't
    seem to remember...
CONSTABLE MACDONALD Mrs. Wilberforce...
MRS. WILBERFORCE Oh, this really is too much.
CONSTABLE MACDONALD Mrs. Wilberforce. Please. Sit down.

She does so

CONSTABLE MACDONALD (CONT'D) What I am about to say will
    come as a surprise to you, but it is vitally important that you pay close
    attention. It would make things a good deal easier for everyone, if you
    would just forget all about this little matter.
MRS. WILBERFORCE Forget about it?
CONSTABLE MACDONALD It really would be for the best.

MRS. WILBERFORCE But... but why?

CONSTABLE MACDONALD It would save me and my colleagues a great deal of embarrassment. Can you imagine the scandal were it to emerge that a master criminal and his gang were right under our very noses, all the time we were looking for them?

MRS. WILBERFORCE But the money? What about the money?

CONSTABLE MACDONALD Keep it.

MRS. WILBERFORCE Keep it?

CONSTABLE MACDONALD Yes, why not? It's all insured. It'll amount to less than a farthing off everyone's premiums.

MRS. WILBERFORCE That's what they said! But Constable, I don't...I don't know what to...

CONSTABLE MACDONALD (*stands up*) Don't think anything of it, Mrs. Wilberforce. Just... keep it to yourself. You know what people are like. They might think you're, ha, ha, making it up! Ha, ha!

MRS. WILBERFORCE Yes...I suppose...I suppose it is all rather fantastical. But it's true, every word of it!

CONSTABLE MACDONALD Oh, I don't doubt that, Mrs. Wilberforce. Nevertheless.

MRS. WILBERFORCE I shan't speak of it again. Thank you, Constable. I really don't know what to say.

CONSTABLE MACDONALD Goodbye, Mrs. Wilberforce! Always a pleasure!

He leaves

Mrs. Wilberforce sits there for a moment, stunned

She suddenly starts

MRS. WILBERFORCE Oh!

She goes to the closet where the men were hiding earlier, opens it, and drags out the cello case. She opens it and stares at the money

MRS. WILBERFORCE (CONT'D) (*in tears*) Oh, General Gordon! Everything's going to be all right!

THE END